MW00323746

Finish What You Start: The Art of Following Through, Taking Action, Executing, & Self-Discipline

By Peter Hollins,
Author and Researcher at
pethollins.com

Table of Contents

Introduction

What exactly is finishing what you start and following through? You have may heard these phrases before, but what do they mean?

To me, they mean making your intentions reality. Too often, we'll say we'll do something, and we might even start it one lucky weekend. But at the first sign of hardship, fatigue, boredom, or busyness, we abandon it all too easily and it sits in our garage (mental, figurative, or literal) for the rest of eternity.

Finishing what you start and following through is breaking through that common loop and taking hold of your life.

My personal experience with finishing what I start has been checkered. One summer, I promised myself that I would carve a wooden canoe, about 12 inches long and 3 inches wide. Not too big, but a sufficient challenge for someone with no woodworking experience. The first week, I made a considerable dent in my wood block. The second week, my hands were sore and the new *Star Wars* movie was out. The third week, I was too busy seeing *Star Wars* again and procrastinating. My wooden canoe wasn't meant to be.

But every time I walked through my garage to my car, the canoe was a damning reminder of my laziness and inability to follow through. It wore on me until I committed myself to finishing it a couple of summers later. You can probably guess what happened. The first week went great, the second week was moderate, and the third week I was already running on fumes.

I was fortunate to learn about temptation bundling some time shortly thereafter, which provided the boost for me to finish my canoe. Briefly, as temptation bundling will be a major theme later in the book, temptation bundling is when you combine an obligatory (and undesirable) task with an instantaneous reward. When you can bribe yourself into working hard, suddenly finishing what you start isn't a massive exercise in willpower—it's the pursuit of something pleasurable, if only by association.

The reward I bundled the canoe carving with was listening to my favorite albums—something we rarely have time for these days. When's the last time you listened to your favorite album from beginning to end without interruption?

Suddenly, a new world was opened to me; if I could make any unpleasant task just pleasant enough by pairing it with something I enjoyed, I could plow my way through just about anything. It was a small realization like this that led me to study the science of following through and executing, despite the human brain's instinctual resistance to doing so. How can we circumvent our worst instincts and get things done when we want, without the specter of a deadline over our heads? How can we pay attention to our attention and do that what is most difficult—live with supreme discomfort?

I'd like to think I've come up with great systems for myself that can be widely applied for just about any context. There are many tactics in this book—I don't use all of them all of the time, but most of them will work for most people. As usual, I wrote this book for myself and am glad and proud to be able to share my findings. I hope they are helpful and help you accomplish exactly what you want. At least, I hope they force you to listen to your favorite albums from time to time—a win in itself!

Chapter 1. Stop Thinking, Just Execute

Esther has thought about it a million times. Stuck in a dead-end desk job for the last six years, she has fantasized about not having to deal with the monotony of paperwork, not having to report to a demanding boss, and not having to leave her two-year-old son at the daycare center every day.

And exactly how were such fantasies supposed to be realized when she had to earn a living to make ends meet for her family? She had the answer: she figured she'd start her own baking business right at home.

It was all just a fantasy, a thought she'd conjure to get her through difficult days at work. But one day, something felt different. For some reason, she finally decided—she's going for it. After all, baking was her one true passion. For years, she'd been baking cakes and cookies for her friends, who all said she should think of turning it into a business, so maybe it wasn't such a bad idea, right?

So began Esther's quest to open her baking business. She didn't quit her job just yet but filed for a two-week vacation leave to start testing the waters. *First*, she thought, *research*. She figured that she needed to get this business thing all figured out in her head first, before she took any further step forward. The more prepared and planned she was, the better. She intended to research everything there is to know about starting such a venture, from recipes to finance management. She also planned to survey her friends and the entire neighborhood to get a feel of the market needs. It was all starting to take shape in her head.

Unfortunately, whatever took shape in Esther's head stayed there and never found its way out.

The thought of having to learn everything about how to start and run a baking business from scratch overwhelmed Esther so much that she was paralyzed from taking any action in that direction. Taxes, business filings, leases? All she wanted to do was bake!

When her vacation days started, she always found things to do other than what she had initially planned. She spent her days sleeping in, doting on her son, busying herself with "home projects," and catching up with her friends and neighbors—and not even to ask them for marketing input. She was too worried that if she started telling people about wanting to start a business they might think she was too ambitious for her level of talent, expect her to fail, or, worse, expect her to succeed. She couldn't deal with the idea of expectations hanging over her head.

Two weeks thus came and went, and all Esther managed to do was put the "vacation" in vacation leave. As she headed back to work, the thought of running her own baking business kept on replaying in her head, still more a fantasy than a plan. She had a feeling she'd continue to think about it, several million times more.

What Is Following Through?

What do you suppose went wrong in Esther's situation? Did she lack focus? Self-discipline? Action? Persistence?

If you say she lacked all of the above, you're pointing to actually just one concept: following through.

Following through is related to focus, self-discipline, action, and persistence, but it is not synonymous to any of them. Rather, it is a composite of all of them—a bit like how those big Japanese anime robots come to be formed by the fusion of smaller individual robot parts. *Power Rangers*, or *Voltron*, to be specific. And much like how each smaller robot forms a different body part in the big robot, so too does each of these four elements—focus, self-discipline, action, and persistence—correspond to a body part that, when pieced with the others, forms the whole of following through.

The head: focus. Following through involves having focus. It's akin to the head because it is focus that keeps your head in the game and your eyes on the prize. Focus guides your thoughts in figuring out how to follow through and directs your actions toward achieving your vision. See, following through is not just about exerting effort; it's about exerting effort that's concentrated on a single goal. With focus, no effort is wasted. What's followed is a single line of sight, so what's pursued is the single most direct way toward a goal.

Going back to Esther's situation, had she been focused on her dream of starting a business, she would've structured her free time better, scheduling activities in view of realizing that dream.

The spine: self-discipline. The spine of following through, self-discipline, is what enables you to get your head down and work when you need to, even if you don't want to. It's the ability to control yourself so that you retain focus on what needs to be done, despite the temptations and distractions you may encounter. This element is essential to following through because it's what gives you the power to regulate your own thoughts, feelings, and actions toward ends that are meaningful to you. Without self-discipline, you wouldn't be able to consistently exert effort on something until it's done, which is what following through is all about.

As the head is continuous with the spine, so is focus continuous with self-discipline. If you are focused on what you need to do, self-discipline will naturally follow. Likewise, if you are self-disciplined, it will be easier for you to focus on what needs to be done and avoid distractions. Self-discipline, like the spine, keeps you upright so you don't slump into a mess.

If Esther had enough self-discipline, she would've been able to resist using all her free time just for leisure. There's nothing wrong with catching up on some sleep or spending time with your loved ones, but if all your days are spent doing just those and none of productive work, then balance is lost. Leisure is an important part of life, but if it's excessive and takes the place of reasonable productivity, then it becomes a vice.

The hands and feet: action. Action, the hands and feet of following through, means prioritizing execution and simple motion. This is what makes following through more than just having focus and self-discipline. Following through is an intention that's been translated into action. It is action that will move things in the real world and take you from Point A to Point B—that is, from where you are now to where the fulfillment of your goals lies. It is the visible aspect of following through, the one that's actually observed, measured, and evaluated against your goals. Action is thus crucial to the execution of your plans and the realization of your goals, for without it, plans remain abstract and goals remain dreams.

Had Esther acted on even just the first part of her plan, research, she would've at least inched her way toward realizing the dream business she had in mind.

The heart: persistence. Finally, at the heart of following through is persistence. Persistence is firmly sticking to something for a prolonged period of time, even as you encounter things that try to *unstick* you. It's the tenacity to adhere to a course of action even in the face of obstacles. It is not enough to just start; you need stick with it until it's done. Following through is about having enough heart to keep pushing even in the face of obstacles, distractions, and setbacks. Many of the goals worth aiming for in life call for not just a sprint but a marathon. If your heart is not fit enough to run the length of it, then you will find yourself stopping halfway through and giving up before you reach the finish line.

Did Esther have the persistence to see her dream through? It seems this question isn't even available to ask in Esther's case, as the question of persistence can only arise if one has in fact taken enough action to get to encounter several roadblocks over an extended period of time. Since Esther stopped before she even began, the question of persistence wasn't even in the equation for her.

So there you have it—the individual parts focus, self-discipline, action, and persistence all combine to be the super-robot called following through and finishing what you start. It's gratifying and fulfilling to be able to pull together focus, self-discipline, action, and persistence within ourselves and get to watch our dreams be turned into reality as a result of it.

But if following through is so awesome, why don't we all just do it all the time? The short answer is because it's hard. The long answer (which also explains why it's hard) is detailed below.

Why Don't We Follow Through?

When it comes to thinking up what we want to do, what we need to do, or what other people need to do, we're usually experts. Our ideas run wild, the blueprints in our heads get magically written out with not much effort, and the mental picture of us living our dreams comes into sharp focus faster than we can say "cheese!"

But when it comes to actually getting off our butts and following through with action, we're usually not only amateurs but also unwilling participants. When it comes down to it, we often couldn't find the focus, self-discipline, action, and persistence needed to get the job done.

Sometimes we go into the battle without our heads or our spines; other times we lack our hands and feet or our hearts. We think we could just call on these parts to get together when we need them to, but we arrive at the battleground only to discover that it's never as easy as we thought it would be.

The excitement and enthusiasm with which we thought out all our dreams and plans fizzle out as soon as we realize the amount of hard work we need to put in to turn those dreams into reality, to bring those plans into life. We don't follow through, and it's not for lack of ability or intelligence, no.

We don't follow through for two main reasons: we have an entire selection of (1) *inhibiting tactics* and/or (2) *psychological roadblocks* that hinder us from finishing what we start. We'll cover each of those in turn below.

Inhibiting Tactics

Inhibiting tactics refer to our schemes for misusing time and effort, with the end result of our being held back from following through. These are ways we sabotage ourselves, sometimes consciously. These tactics, which include (1) setting bad goals, (2) procrastination, (3) indulging in temptations and distractions, and (4) poor time management, inhibit us from maximizing the time and energy we have toward productive ends.

Setting bad goals. One way we handicap ourselves from following through is by setting bad goals, such as those that are too abstract or downright impossible. Setting bad goals is like buying the wrong map for a road trip; it prevents us from following through because the directions are skewed and confusing. It eventually causes us to lose patience and will to keep on in our journey, which we often end up abandoning halfway through.

When our goals are too abstract, we find ourselves lost as to what needs to be done in order to reach them. For example, if we say our goal is to be healthier and yet don't even specify what we mean by "healthier," we're less likely to take steps toward accomplishing it. We want to follow through, but we don't know how.

When our goals are too high or unrealistic for any mortal to reach, we find ourselves looking up at an impossibly high ladder without rungs. The beauty of this is that no one would be able to accuse us of not trying hard enough to climb, because there are no rungs in the first place. We are absolved from the guilt of not following through. Take for instance a plant manager aiming to double manufacturing output despite real logistical limitations.

Since the goal is impossible to achieve anyway, whether he follows through or not wouldn't make a difference—and so he's saved from both the trouble of having to follow through and the guilt from not doing so.

Procrastination. This is one of the most widely used tactics in the book. We are somehow exceptionally talented at delaying work until we absolutely need to do it, until the very last minute. In fact, we're so talented at delaying work that we could convince others (and even ourselves) that we're already working even when we're not.

One way we procrastinate is with endless planning. We plan all the details of our task, and once we're done planning, we decide that either the plan needs revising or the task itself needs to be scrapped. Then we plan for a new task, and so on—all the while conveniently unaware of the fact that all the planning we're doing is also a form of procrastination. Ultimately, it's something best referred to as *productive procrastination* because it feels like you're getting somewhere, but you're really just moving in place.

If we can get away with putting off a task at the moment, we tend to do so because it's easy, comfortable, and stress-free. This is how a lot of would've-been success stories get to be just that—would've been. A lifetime string of "laters" ends up being woven into the noose of "never."

Temptations and distractions. The road of following through would be easy enough to tread, without delay, if it were like a hallway with blank walls on either side. If you didn't have a choice, you might very well put your head down and work, work, work. But no. This road is lined with all sorts of shiny trinkets, glittering detour signs, and inviting rest stops. Temptations and distractions come aplenty these days, with something as simple as a red notification alert on our phone screens flooding our brains with feel-good chemicals that, in turn, keep us glued to our phones even longer.

Take for example a marketing officer tasked to develop a campaign to promote a new product. She is well aware of the research she needs to do, the reports she needs to write, the presentations she needs to start prepping. But instead of following through and retaining focus so she gets things done faster, her hours are riddled by Snapchat conversations, YouTube binges, and endless Instagram scrolls. Eventually, the research may get done, the reports may get written, and the presentations may be prepped, but such are not likely to reflect her true potential.

But of course, we cannot rid the world of temptations and distractions. After all, they're not the main problem. The main problem is that we lack the know-how to properly deal with them. While they may come aplenty on either side of the road, there are two ways we can still manage the situation through (1) strategic avoidance and (2) healthy, moderate use.

First, we may implement strategies to avoid temptations and distractions. For example, if we're distracted by frequent notifications from social media, we may schedule blocks of time during which we're logged out from our social media accounts while we focus on our work.

Second, we may deal with temptations and distractions in a healthy and productive way. We don't need to deprive ourselves of tempting and enjoyable leisure activities for the rest of our lives just so we could follow through on our goals. In fact, we're not supposed to.

Giving ourselves a well-deserved break by indulging in activities we find enjoyable would help recharge us so we could function better. The key is in having the discipline enough to indulge on those activities in a healthy way. For instance, we may periodically reward ourselves with a 10-minute break, during which we log back in and check on our social media accounts, after we accomplish a set amount of work.

Poor time management. "So much to do, and not enough time to do it." How many times have you heard these words spoken by a colleague, a family member, or the person looking back at you in the mirror? And how many times could you see that it's not time they lacked, but the ability to use their time productively? We all have the same amount of time in the day.

Time management is the practice of using time in a way that maximizes productivity and efficiency. Good time management involves not only the ability to schedule tasks, but also the insight and good judgment to recognize which tasks are best done when. Moreover, it requires having the self-discipline to do tasks as initially planned and the focus to organize resources accordingly. With good time management, a schedule is cleverly organized and then promptly followed, so tasks get done as planned.

On the other hand, bad time management involves a lack of planning, organization, focus, and self-discipline. We forget, overlook, or miscalculate tasks in terms of how much time they'd require for completion, leading to a domino effect that messes up the rest of our plans. We fail to foresee and provide for the resources we need for the activities we've planned, leading to delays and cancellations. We fail to prioritize our activities, instead choosing to spend our time doing nonessential tasks, leading to unsuccessful endeavors (plus maybe a scolding glare from our boss).

Life in the 21st century is challenging our ability to maintain work-life balance like no other time before. With technology allowing more work hours as well as more entertainment options than ever, we no longer seem to find 24 hours enough to fit in everything we need and want to do in a day. With such demands and lifestyles, poor time management has become the norm, and good time management is a superpower only the enlightened have seemed to master.

And if we can't even manage our time when it comes to our day-to-day tasks, how could we expect to find time to follow through on our bigger life plans?

Psychological Roadblocks

Psychological roadblocks refer to the internal, often unconscious mechanisms in our psyches that act as barriers to following through. Among these mechanisms are (1) laziness and lack of discipline, (2) fear of judgment, rejection, and failure, (3) perfectionism out of insecurity, and (4) lack of self-awareness. These psychological roadblocks operate internally to inhibit external action, thus preventing us from following through.

Laziness and lack of discipline. The reason we don't follow through can sometimes be as simple as being too lazy and lacking the discipline to do so. Our laziness hinders us from getting off the couch and working on the important tasks that will get us closer to our goals. Our lack of discipline sees us squandering our time to distractions and temptations. We may get our calendars planned out, our to-do lists ready, and everything else we need prepared, but somehow we lack the willpower and discipline within us to just start, just do, and just keep pushing. We see the sacrifice, however small, we would have to make, and we decide that it's not worth it.

Willpower is the energy that activates our bodies, while discipline is the focus that directs that energy so that we're constantly moving toward our goals. If we don't find a way to turn our willpower and discipline on, our bodies would simply continue to be in their inactive state, never following through.

Fear of judgment, rejection, and failure. Imagine Lara, a volunteer for a local organization helping provide education for less fortunate children. She has an idea for a fundraising campaign that will bring in more sponsors. She plans what she needs to do and researches who she needs to talk to in order to make things happen.

But before she even makes the first call to get the ball rolling, her breath catches. She hesitates and thinks, *What if I organize this campaign but nobody signs up for it? What if our community leaders back my idea but it winds up being a flop? What if we'd end up spending more money than we actually gain?* So she drops the idea entirely and immediately starts breathing easier.

What stopped Lara from following through was her fear of judgment, rejection, and failure. To her, not following through was an act of self-preservation, a way to save herself from the pain of failure. Since she never asked for anything, she never got rejected. Since she never went after a goal, no one could say she failed at it.

Fear of judgment, rejection, and failure thus paralyzes us from following through. We think that by abstaining from action, we cancel out the possibility of producing any output that might be subject to evaluation or judgment. And if we can't be evaluated or judged, we also can't be rejected. If we don't try to go for things, especially things that challenge us, then we can't fail. However, these are ruinous distortions in reasoning. By not acting and not following through, we have already judged and rejected ourselves even before we've started. We have already failed the moment we decided not to try.

Perfectionism out of insecurity. Paul has been planning to apply for promotion for several years now. He has been putting in the effort to upgrade his professional knowledge and skills, attending seminars, taking certification exams, and enrolling in post-graduate classes. He wants his résumé to be perfect so that when he does apply for promotion, he can be sure he'll get it. For Paul, it was either perfection or nothing.

Several more years passed, and he's still never applied for a higher position. His credentials didn't feel good enough to him, and it never did. His perfectionism, born out of his fear and insecurity that he wasn't good enough, was what prevented Paul from following through. Instead of taking action that will move him forward, he focused his energy on overplanning and striving for perfection, ultimately leading to stagnation. To the outside world, it may have seemed that Paul was a busy bee working toward his goals, but in reality he was internally inhibited by his perfectionism from truly following through.

Lack of self-awareness. Finally, lack of self-awareness could also be a psychological barrier against following through. Because we're so often afraid of making mistakes and venturing past our comfort zones, we never get to learn the fullest extent of what we can do. Thus, many of our interests, passions, and talents remain hidden to us forever. And not knowing our true capacities, we remain convinced that we will never make it, even if we tried. So we don't follow through on our plans and, in so doing, trap ourselves in a lifetime of stagnation.

What's more, we don't even realize we've fallen into the trap of stagnation because we also lack the self-awareness that we're not following through. We continue living our busy lives, content with the idea that we can't possibly be working harder than we already are. But if we strip our lives with the little bits and bobs we busy ourselves with and take a long hard look at the big picture, we then realize that we've been avoiding following through on things that really matter.

So there you have it—the list of reasons why we don't follow through. We start with excitement and enthusiasm but end up with excuses and explanations. We start with anticipation but end up with alibis. And all too often, we don't bother looking past what's in front of us because what's in front of us is easy and convenient. A part of us doesn't want to know what's possible beyond that because we're afraid to want it and to have to do the hard work that will get us there.

But take courage for a moment, and for the sake of your personal growth and happiness, consider how your life would be different if you made following through a habit.

What if We Do Follow Through?

Following through is the more difficult path, but the benefits it can yield make the journey worth the struggle. If you develop the habit of following through, you'll be able to increase your productivity, maximize every opportunity, and realize your fullest potentials. Your academic and career goals will be real guideposts in your life instead of just being pipe dreams and ending up as frustrations.

Being a person who follows through will also improve your relationships. You'll find that as you consistently keep your promises, you'll gain and retain the trust of your supervisors, your colleagues, and your staff. More importantly, you'll be building better relationships with your spouse, your children, and your friends. They know they can trust your word because they've seen you act on your plans and deliver on your promises.

What's more, following through will help you build a better relationship with yourself. Following through forces you to be in touch with your own wants, needs, capacities, and fears more intimately, so you get to take charge of your own life instead of being just a slave to your unconscious fears and society's pressures on you.

In summary, following through is the powerful combination of focus, self-discipline, action, and persistence. It's the force that drives you toward higher professional achievements, better relationships, and greater personal satisfaction.

However, both tactics-based and psychologically-based roadblocks can often hinder you from consistently following through on your dreams and goals. You may have the passion and motivation to do something at first, but the fire within you is likely to die down somewhere along the way. To reignite it, you must first understand what's holding you back, then equip yourself with the right tactics and psychological tools to help you follow through on the things you start.

Recall the story of Esther told at the beginning of this chapter. She took a leave in the hopes of getting to start on her own business, but she failed to follow through because she was tempted to indulge in pleasurable distractions and was taken by her fear of rejection and failure. Instead of using the time she had to set realistic goals and follow through on building the life of her dreams, she ended up returning to a life she didn't enjoy living.

Imagine if Esther was aware of the barriers that were keeping her from following through. Suppose she responded by using the right tactics and psychological tools to counter such barriers and eventually succeeded in running a home-based bakery business. Every day, she'd be waking up excited to get to work with something she's passionate about. She'd get to spend every day near her son and watch him grow. She'd be living the life she had only dreamed of.

Take a moment to consider the story of your own life. Are you following through on what you really want in your life? Or are you constantly falling victim to the tactics and psychological barriers that hinder you from doing so?

If you answered the latter, then read on. The following pages will equip you with the tools you need and show you the way toward developing in yourself the all-important power of following through.

Takeaways:

- The art of following through is something that allows you to create the life that you actually want instead of settling for the life you currently have.
- It can be said to be composed of four parts: focus, self-discipline, action, and persistence—all equally important.
- However, it's not just as easy as knowing you have to do it and thus doing it. There are powerful reasons we don't finish what we start and follow through very

often. These reasons can generally be split into two camps: inhibiting tactics and psychological roadblocks.

- Inhibiting tactics are the ways we plan against ourselves without even realizing it. They include (1) setting bad goals, (2) procrastination, (3) indulging in temptations and distractions, and (4) poor time management.

- Psychological roadblocks are the ways we don't follow through because we are unconsciously protecting ourselves. These include (1) laziness and lack of discipline, (2) fear of judgment, rejection, and failure, (3) perfectionism out of insecurity, and (4) lack of self-awareness.

Chapter 2: Staying Hungry

What drives you to follow through and finish what you start? How can you remain motivated?

Let's consider a woman named Sally. Sally is an idealist so she started a charity to benefit impoverished people. What she did not anticipate was the influx of challenges that came along with her endeavor. She did not realize that working in a nonprofit setting still counts as business and that her work would involve far more business than just helping people.

Whenever she encountered a challenge in procuring funding, competing with other charities for donations and grants, and creating marketing to incite interest in her cause, she felt overwhelmed. "Why is it so hard to get people to care about other people!?" she asked herself.

Pretty soon, Sally became completely disinterested in her work—it just carried with it too many negative feelings and associations. She hated writing grant letters and attending charity events. It took only a few months for her to give up on a cause that she cared deeply about. Other people wondered why she stopped working for something that meant so much to her.

A key to Sally's failure was her inability to anticipate and plan for negative aspects of her foundation. She imagined doing more to help people and working less to procure funding. Because she relied solely on her goals to give her the motivation to follow through, she did not give herself anything to actually help her defeat the negative aspects of the business side of her foundation.

The true problem that Sally had, however, was failing to find a true source of motivation. She needed to have found a true source of motivation to help carry through the discouraging effects of the negatives. By creating a balance between her dream, the positives, and the negatives, the negatives would have been acceptable obstacles in pursuit of her grand goal. She could have also kept her motivation alive by reminding herself of why she undertook this project in the first place and how each thing she did, even the tasks she hated, led to the fulfillment of her idealistic dream.

Sally is a great example of how you can't just count on your passion for something to lead you to follow through.

Sometimes we just don't care about what we are doing, and thus we don't follow through. We lose steam because of disinterest. That's understandable. But even caring about something is not always the key to following through. Sometimes, even for things we care about, we still can't follow through because we lack a drive to push us forward.

This lack of drive is caused by a massive disconnect between three important aspects: (1) what the things we care about represent, (2) the positive benefits we receive from our actions, and (3) the negative consequences we can avoid related to our causes. When we lose steam, we aren't tied closely enough to any of those aspects, which come together to create *motivation*.

What is motivation? Things that really matter to you and are near and dear to your heart. Things that make you actually want to work toward your goal. Things that not only drive you, but also discourage you from giving up. On top of that, you have to minimize negative consequences involved with your work and simultaneously maximize the positive benefits that you receive.

There are many ways to define the concept of motivation, but an effective framework to view them through is *external* and *internal* motivations.

External Motivators

External motivators entail using sources besides yourself as motivation to do something. They are other people or circumstances that drive you to action. You are doing something to avoid a negative circumstance or earn a positive circumstance from people and things outside of you.

More typically, external motivators are about avoiding negative consequences. For example, you might be trying to avoid disappointing your family by failing, so you are determined to succeed. You might be afraid of getting fired, so you act with aplomb. A majority of these motivators are punishments or negative consequences that you are desperate to avoid. The only positive external motivation is self-bribery.

Still, you can get a lot of mileage out of external motivators if you make them work to your advantage. Driving yourself to avoid a negative consequence can serve as an excellent push to do something. No one wants to suffer. If you know that not following through will result in some sort of suffering, you will do anything to avoid that negative consequence. Therefore, you feel as if you have no choice but to follow through.

Accountability partners. Accountability partners are people who hold you accountable. This is a person that you commit to something with. This person lets you know when you need to do things, and he or she chides you when you want to give up. Then he or she gets on your case for not following through.

Since you want to avoid disappointing this person, you are more likely to act. You rely on this person to give you the external motivation to avoid shame so you become accountable for your actions and your goal to avoid his or her negative feedback. You may also become accountable in order to avoid letting this person down, as he or she counts on you to complete the goal with him or her.

Accountability group. An accountability group can be more effective than a single partner. By having multiple people holding you accountable, you face the possibility of exponential shame—the shame and disappointment of multiple people building on top of each other is a horrible feeling that you will want to avoid. Plus, you will still have people to hold you accountable should one person drop out of the race. It can be hard to rely on a single partner's commitment, but a group is much steadier in its pressure. Having more people to answer to and to guide you can help you stay on track to avoid shame.

Putting money down. The risk of losing money is another motivator that you can use to your advantage. A good example of this is an expensive gym membership fee that makes you want to go to the gym more often. You don't want to waste money, so you go to the gym just to make that fee you paid worthwhile.

Another example is paying a lot of money for a course. You want to finish the course because you paid so much for it and you consider it a shame to just waste that fee. By investing in something monetarily upfront and even slightly before you feel ready, you'll be pushed to follow through to avoid wasting and losing money. The primary operator here is guilt for spending money on something that you never used or did.

You can take monetary investment motivators to the next level by hiring a coach or trainer of some type. This is the next level because paying someone money to hold you accountable combines both monetary investments and accountability partners. Now you have two reasons not to quit or back out of your commitment. You don't want to waste money or hear about how you have failed from a disappointed accountability partner.

Finally, you can give someone money and then tell them not to give it to you until you complete something. When you give a friend

$500 and instruct them not to return it to you until you complete your tasks, you'll quickly discover just how much your work ethic is worth to you. If $500 is not enough, up the ante next time to make it truly something you'll work toward.

Self-bribery. A final external motivator is to bribe yourself. This is where you promise yourself a reward if you follow through. Therefore, you let that reward drive you and surmount your difficulties. For example, you might know that you can take your dream beach vacation if you save your money wisely and earn enough to have spare. Keeping the emotions of the beach vacation can be powerful reminders every time you want to spend your money.

External motivations are mostly about avoiding pain, so figure out what pains you are avoiding or can create for yourself. Then let your urge to avoid those pains drive you. Avoiding negative social emotions works well because no one wants to feel shame, guilt, or rejection. Use your fear of negative social emotions to carry you through a project or commitment to the very end.

Internal Motivators

Internal motivators are about what you *want*, as opposed to avoiding a negative consequence or punishment.

If you are motivated by avoiding a negative consequence, but you realize at some point that maybe negative consequence won't actually kill you so you can deal with it, there goes your motivation—you'll simply deal with the consequences sometimes.

In some cases, relying on external motivators and fear does not work as well as going after the things you love and want. Therefore, internal motivators are often better sources of motivation than external ones. We can view it thusly: if you are driven by fear or face a substantial negative consequence, external motivation is ideal, while internal motivation is more suitable if you know what you want and there is little to fear.

Internal motivators are your "why" for taking action and putting in effort. Think of a donkey walking forward to reach the carrot. Internal motivators are the carrot, while external motivators are the stick. External motivators drive you forward out of fear of something unpleasant, while internal motivators make you feel that reaching your goal is going to give you a big reward and lots of pleasant benefits.

The more internal motivations you can articulate, the more motivated you will be to follow through and finish. Ask the following questions to determine how you will benefit, then let your desire for those benefits drive you forward. Internal motivations tend to be more uniform because they speak to people's universal desires and needs.

What are you getting out of this? Maybe you are getting money or a sense of happiness and fulfillment in life. You are getting closer to a goal, which can mean a lot in terms of benefits.

How will your life change or benefit? You may be able to get a better home or a nicer car if you earn more money. Or you may be able to recover from depression and ultimate sadness by attaining a higher sense of fulfillment.

How will your family benefit? Your family means a lot to you, so let them motivate you. Imagine the smiles on their faces as you give them a better life and make them proud. Imagine getting your kids better school clothes, living in a safer neighborhood, and being able to afford private school and college.

What impact will you have on others? Perhaps you will become a role model for some people, which in turn will make you feel important and good about yourself. Perhaps you can donate to charity or gift needy people with clothes and shoes come winter. Perhaps you can donate money to erect new structures in your community that will be named after you.

What positive emotions will you get? Consider the happiness, pride, and self-esteem you will reap from your goal's ultimate completion. After all, this may be the root of all philanthropic efforts.

How will your actions lead to your long-term and short-term goals? Are you accomplishing steps toward your goals? Think of the things you must do to finish a novel, for example, such as research and actual word count. Then think of the steps you take each day toward those goals.

Using internal motivators in your daily life can really help you follow through with every task you have to complete. Even when the going gets tough and you contemplate giving up, finishing what you start is way easier when you are focused on how your world will benefit. So whenever you have to do something that you hate, think of how it will bring you closer to your goals. Or whenever you find yourself bored or tired while working on your goals, consider how great you will feel when you finish. Every day, review your goals and why you want to complete them. Then let that fill you with motivation to drive you forward toward project completion.

Answer the above questions and consider writing them down somewhere. Review the answers periodically to remind yourself why you want to change or improve your status quo.

Understand Opportunity Cost

Following through and finishing what you start will always call for sacrifice.

You have to spend money, expend effort, and give up time that you could use for doing things you love in order to commit to things you have to complete. Since by definition no one likes sacrifice, sometimes the looming shadow of a sacrifice will overshadow your goals—unless you create motivators powerful enough to overpower your sense of sacrifice and make each sacrifice seem worthwhile.

Everything in life is an *opportunity cost*, which means that everything you do will call for something from you. Every act takes away time or effort that could be committed to something else. Learning to play the guitar means solitary hours of drilling scales, chords, and dealing with painful calluses on your fingers. Going to college entails getting up early and heading to a boring lecture and spending hours doing homework. Are you ready to make the trade-off?

If the opportunity cost is too expensive for you to want to pay it, then you will not follow through. Therefore, you must find a motivator that drives you to accept the opportunity cost. If you don't feel motivated enough to pay that cost, then you are guaranteed to lose steam and give up.

Therefore, there are two ways to solve this problem. The first is that your motivation must be even stronger and more salient in order to make you ignore these opportunity costs and the things you are missing out on. The motivation must mean more to you than the things you sacrifice to make you feel that this is all worth it.

The second solution is to make your sacrifices smaller. This means that there is less pain associated with getting things done. In both cases, the cost-benefit analysis must be significantly weighed in favor of the benefit—but the first method manipulates the benefit, while the second method manipulates the cost.

An example of this is giving give up your weekly Friday night out with friends to go to a late-night history class. This class is essential to getting the degree you need to break into your dream career. But you sure do love your night out with friends. To use the first solution, your desire to get into this career and better your life and feel proud of yourself must outweigh how much you love Friday nights out. You must keep in mind that your life will drastically change for the better if you can resist a few Friday nights. Otherwise, you will find the conflict too great to overcome and you will quit the class in favor of your friends.

Let's apply the second solution for the same results. Instead of just giving up on your Friday night out, schedule a different night or drum up the energy to go out after class and spend just a little less time with your friends every Friday night. You're turning a full sacrifice into a compromised sacrifice. The end result is a compromise that makes it possible to keep doing what you want while also working on your goals.

When faced with opportunity cost and potential sacrifice, keep in mind that your life can't continue 100% as you want it to—but if you focus on increasing the benefit or minimizing the sacrifice, you can continue progress toward your goals while staying motivated and not listless.

Keep Your Motivation on Your Mind

Internal and external motivators are great ways to fuel the productivity and commitment required for following through. But they won't do anything for you if they are out of sight and out of mind.

According to *Psychological Science,* people are more inclined to follow through if they are exposed to stimuli that remind them of their motivators. Seeing or hearing their motivators can drive them to maintain motivation. In other words, sometimes the simplest solutions work best: constant reminders will keep you on track because our minds can only fixate on so many things.

Additionally, Katherine Milkman of the University of Pennsylvania developed the hypothesis that reminders through association could aid people in remembering goals and following through with them.

To confirm this hypothesis, she conducted a study whose participants were asked to complete an hour-long computer task. They were promised compensation as well as a dollar donated to the local food bank. They were asked to make sure their donations were made by picking up paperclips when they got their compensation. The control group was told this and then thanked for their time. The test group was told that the paper clips would be waiting by an elephant statue.

It turned out that 74% of the group told about the elephant statue remembered to get their paper clips at the end of the study. Only 42% of the members of the other group remembered to do this. Having the visual cue of the elephant statue actually made it easier for students to remember to complete the simple task. When students saw the unusual statue, it sparked their memories far more than ordinary-looking notes.

On top of that, Rogers and Milkman discovered that having very noticeable cues worked better than cues that did not stand out. For example, a written reminder did not remind study participants as well as a visual cue such as one of the aliens from *Toy Story.*

Therefore, the best way to make motivators work for you is to expose yourself to them often. You can use cues to help prompt you to keep your motivation in mind and thus to follow through. However, these cues also need to stand out to you.

For instance, use loud, vivid images that you can't ignore, or employ other senses and include sounds, textures, and scents. Include a picture on your desk of your child to remind you to keep working toward your dream for a better financial future for your family—but make the picture frame smell of your child's shampoo or your spouse's perfume or cologne. To emphasize, we aren't just talking about visual aids of putting Post-its everywhere—the cues we can use can be spread across our five senses in imaginative and creative ways.

However, be sure to move and change these cues around every few days so that you do not become too accustomed to them and start to ignore them as part of the background noise of your life.

Finally, you can also write your motivators down every few days with different phrasing. Again, be sure to change them up to avoid getting too used to them. The act of creating the cue each repeatedly helps to keep the motivation firm and fresh in your mind.

Takeaways:

- How do we stay hungry and motivated? By delving deep and really asking what internal and external motivators you have at your disposal—a task that is rarely performed.
- External motivators are when we leverage other people, places, and things to push us into action. For the most part, these are when we want to avoid negative consequences involving other people, places, and things. These methods include accountability partners and groups, putting money down upfront, and self-bribery.
- Internal motivators are when we look at how we stand to benefit and improve our lives. These are universal needs, drives, and desires that are easy to lose track of. The easy way to find these is to answer a set of questions that directly asks things such as *how am I going to benefit from this* and *how does my life stand to improve from this*? It's only through answering these questions that you realize what you are neglecting.
- Anything we want to accomplish has an associated opportunity cost. We must

sacrifice, even if we are sacrificing our ability to lie on the couch and watch television. We can deal with this mental obstacle by playing with the cost-benefit ratio so the cost is minimized or the benefit is maximized.

- Motivation has been shown to work best when we are reminded of it—otherwise, out of sight, out of mind. Thus, you should have cues you're your motivations all around you—but make sure to keep them distinct and memorable, use all five senses (even taste), and make sure to change and switch them periodically to avoid growing used to them and forgetting them.

Chapter 3: Create a Manifesto

You will face forks in the road where you must deliberate between following through or giving up. Instead of having to make the hard decision and reach deep into your willpower toolbag every single time, having rules for yourself can help you decide which direction to take whenever you reach the fork.

We've been told since we were young that we have to follow rules. Well, this time we can choose our own rules that will ultimately help us accomplish exactly what we want.

Rules can generally be called *mental models*, which can be critical to follow-through. This is because they create a set way that you have to make every decision, no exceptions. With your decisions already made for you by your rules, you thus make decisions automatically and you no longer have room to make the wrong decision based on waning willpower and self-discipline, which is to give up.

Rules hold you accountable so that you are not winging it every day but instead are guided. Use your rules to guide your worldview and your daily actions. Let them make every decision for you.

A good example of a rule is to always complete two tasks on your to-do list for your goal every day. It's simply unacceptable to not do this—you have to complete the steps no matter what. As a result, you'll find that you make progress toward your goal, even when you don't want to. The choice was out of your hands. Deciding to work each day is not your decision to make; it has already been made for you by your rule, and thus you have no choice but to do it.

Consider an example of when John, a writer, doesn't use the rule of always completing two steps on his to-do list.

In the morning, he is excited and thinks, "After work, I will go home and start writing my novel! I will write two chapters." Then he goes to work and grows fatigued and loses his inspiration slowly but surely throughout the day. By the time he gets home, all he wants to do is watch *Gossip Girl*. So since he does not have this rule in place, he fails to write. He has made zero progress and is far from his goal. The sense of guilt that plagues him is horrible. As he goes to bed, he vows to himself that he will make up for the lost progress by writing four chapters tomorrow.

What do you think will happen then? He comes home tired and defeated again. He lets the fact that work drains him become his excuse for not writing. Moreover, since he faces the monumental task of writing four chapters today, it feels impossible to start on. If he didn't have energy for two chapters the night before, he certainly won't have the energy for four chapters tonight. He gets overwhelmed and doesn't write at all. It seems as if he will never finish this novel because he always finds some excuse to let himself off of the hook from actually writing.

He gave himself too much choice and leeway and thus allowed self-sabotage all too easily.

Now let's consider if John applied the rule every day, which is black and white and doesn't care about fatigue. No matter how tired and uninspired he feels, he knows that he has to write two chapters a night after work, no exceptions and no excuses. So when he gets home, he looks at his computer and he feels tempted to just go watch TV and conserve his energy by being lazy. But because he follows a rule in his life, he can't break it and so he has to write. In fact, he plans for it all day because he knows it's coming. He sits down and tackles the two chapters and goes to bed exhausted but contented and proud of himself. He has made significant progress on his novel. Pretty soon, he is done with his novel and the feeling of accomplishment is worth the energy he had to spend on the novel when he was drained after work.

Rules help you follow through because they limit your vision. When you are robbed of your decision-making power—the same power that leads you to fiddle with social media when important tasks need to be done—then your hands are tied and following through is the only choice you have.

This chapter is about creating a set of rules, collectively a *manifesto*, for you to follow every time you come across a fork in the road. They push and guide you into the right direction and avoid depleting the willpower you do have. Here are a few ideas for you.

Rule 1: Evaluate Yourself

Rule 1 is to ask yourself, "If not for laziness or fear, would I be giving up?" This makes it very clear to yourself that you are not acting out of a lack of ability or talent, but rather you are just taking the easy way out. Is that what you want to admit to yourself? When you face the fact that you are being lazy or fearful head-on, it makes you not want to be that way anymore. It's the kick in the butt that forces you to call yourself lazy/fearful and then drives you to take action.

Realizing that only fear or laziness stands in your way helps you realize how silly that is so you get over it. So before you give up, make it a rule that you always ask yourself if it is laziness or fear that is holding you back from action.

Let's say that you have a goal to make a certain amount of money by delivering so many projects to your clients in a month. But the work is hard and you find yourself losing motivation. You want to stop working and take several days off. Ask yourself, "Am I just being lazy?" That kicks your butt into gear and you take action. You do your work and you feel better about yourself knowing that you are doing the best you can.

Rule 2: Three Tasks Maximum

Rule 2 is to focus on three things a day *maximum*. Only. Tops. Being overwhelmed or disorganized can kill your ability to get things done. Sometimes we can't follow through on what we want because we don't plan smartly. We give ourselves too much to do and we become overwhelmed. But using this rule enables you to plan against that problem by only allowing yourself to focus on three things a day maximum. Plan how to reduce your focus to only three things by deciding on what they are going to be the night before. Prepare to focus only on those things so that you can plan logically and not react emotionally.

One setback you'll face when you attempt to limit yourself to three main tasks a day is differentiation. Specifically, you will need to learn to differentiate between *important* things and *urgent* things. Important things must be done and should make it to your top three, while urgent things are not necessary.

Urgent things will seem important and will cause you stress, but they may not actually be important or take priority. An urgent thing might be making time for a harried client who is rushing you. Meanwhile, getting a project to a client before the deadline is an example of an important task. Everything on your agenda will appear important *and* urgent so you must determine which is which and plan accordingly.

Similarly, differentiate between useless motion that looks busy but gets nothing done and actual action, which is movement toward what you want. Useless motion is shifting papers around your desk, while actual action is using those papers to get work done and make progress on a project. Make what really matters the priority.

How might you use this rule is to set an agenda for yourself? Suppose you have five tasks to do for your business. Two of the tasks are not really important and only appear to be since they are urgent, so you decide to focus on them later.

You pick three tasks to focus on, and you evaluate which one is most important so that you can focus on that first. The night before, look at those three items on your to-do list and determine what steps you will take in actual action to complete those items, starting with the most important one. The next day, take that actual action for your first task, then your second, then your third. Only complete one task at a time and do not multitask. By the close of the workday, you just completed three major tasks at a realistic pace!

Rule 3: Create Limitations and Requirements

Rule 3 is to make actual rules for yourself. Create an actual code of conduct for you to follow in terms of being more disciplined and following through more. Write your code down in detail and then post it in a visible area. While you may not adhere to all of them every day, you at least stand a better chance of follow-through when you actually take the time to think about your code of conduct and write them down.

The rules should focus on creating either *limitations* or *requirements* for what you do each day so that you actually take initiative and get tasks done.

This rule forces you to determine what you really need and want and analyze what you hope to achieve. Basically, you are stopping to check yourself and evaluate how you are progressing toward your ultimate goal. It helps you focus more on your intentions and clarify them, making them an integral part of your work ethic. So when you set out to accomplish something, you have a rule in place to make yourself follow through on the project.

Give yourself five daily limitations and five daily requirements. Make clear statements about what you *cannot* do and what you *must* do.

Limitations are relatively easy to understand. They limit distraction and temptation. As for requirements, understand that you are not Superman or Superwoman, so you can't overload yourself. Instead, work smarter and have five requirements that you can *reasonably* meet. You may not always adhere to this rule, but you at least have some guidance for yourself. In addition, you gain some clarity about what you have cut out for you each day.

An example is to set a limitation that you will not watch more than one hour of TV a day, you will not spend more than an hour on Facebook, and you will not take longer than a one-hour lunch break. Meanwhile, your requirements are that you must read at least 30 pages a day, you must complete at least four hours of work before lunch, and you must complete eight hours of work total by the time you sign out or clock out of work.

Rule 4: Reaffirm Your Intentions

Rule 4 is quite similar to rule 1. This rule comes into play when you are faced with a fork in the road between deciding to follow through or not. This rule seeks to *reaffirm your intentions* by reminding yourself what they are and why you want to achieve them.

When you find yourself deliberating between quitting and following through, ask these three questions to yourself. Better yet, have the answers written somewhere so you can look over again.

"I want..." This is where you state your end goal and how you will benefit from it. What is your reason and motivation? Keep reminding yourself of the external or internal motivators that you have on your side. Remind yourself something like, "I want to be rich."

"I will..." This is where you state how you must reach that end goal and all the work you should be doing to get there. This statement brings your attention back to how necessary it is to complete what you are currently doing and how these tasks tie

into the end goal. The journey is a necessary part of the goal. It helps for you to be very specific in this statement to see what actions you really do have to take. For example, tell yourself, "If I want to be rich, I will need to finish this project and work hard on other projects."

"I won't..." This is where you state what you shouldn't do because that action will impede your progress toward your end goal. There are many things detrimental to your progress, including distractions, temptations, lack of discipline, procrastination, and other destructive or wasteful actions. Tell yourself something like, "If I want to be rich, I won't distract myself with social media and I won't prioritize social media over my work projects."

Let's apply this concept to a potential real-life conundrum that you may encounter. As you work to complete a certification program necessary to get a pay raise at work, you find the volume of work overwhelming and you despise having so little free time on your hands. You contemplate giving up and saying "whatever" to the certification. After all, you have a job, so do you really need to advance yourself anymore?

As you contemplate this, realize that this is the time when you should apply this rule because you have hit a fork in the road of follow-through. You choose to implement the rule and you state three things to yourself:

"I want to make more money at work and be able to afford a nicer home for myself and a future family."

"If I want to have more money and move into a better place, I will finish this certification program in order to get a raise at work."

"If I want to make more money at work and move into a better place, I won't let myself get discouraged and stop doing the work to complete this program or be thrown off track by simple temptations or laziness."

You have just stated your intentions from beginning to end. As you may have noticed, a running theme in this book is that repetition helps follow through, and presence of mind is key. We may have the best intentions, but if we simply forget about them, then what good are they? When you face these questions constantly—your end goal and the steps you must take to reach, as well as the steps you must not take to reach it—it all becomes crystal clear.

Rule 5: Think in Terms of 10-10-10

The next time you feel that you're about to give in to an urge or temptation, stop and ask yourself how you will feel 10 minutes, 10 hours, and 10 days from now. This rule may not seem all that powerful, but it's effective because it forces you to think about your future self and to see how your actions are going to affect yourself in the future—for better or worse. A lot of times, we may know that we are losing willpower or doing something harmful in the moment, but that's not enough to stop us from doing it because we don't have any connection to our future self that will have to deal with the consequences. This rule quickly creates that connection, and that can make the difference between a success or failure of discipline.

Why time intervals of 10 minutes, hours, and days? Because that helps you realize how short-term the pleasure or comfort of a discipline is relative to its long-term consequences. At 10 minutes, you might be feeling good, with perhaps just the initial bit of shame creeping in. After 10 hours, you'll feel mostly shame a regret. Ten days later, you might be consumed by regret having realized some of the negative consequences that your decision or action has had on your pursuit of your long-term goals.

On the other hand, you might apply this rule and realize that a lapse in following through now won't make a difference 10 days into the future. If that's the case, then you can indulge a bit without guilt or shame.

For example, imagine that you apply this rule when deciding whether or not to skip a workout to go to dinner with coworkers. If you've just begun exercising and haven't built it into a consistent habit yet, your decision to skip a single workout might increase the odds of skipping future workouts or stopping working out altogether.

How will you feel in 10 minutes, hours, and days? Ten minutes—good, with a slight tinge of regret, as you can still taste the lasagna or ice cream. The pleasure is still tangible. Ten hours—almost entirely regret, as the pleasure is gone and fleeting, and your diet has been soundly broken. Ten days—100% regret, because the broken discipline is now completely meaningless and but a faint memory. The lasagna does not have a lasting benefit, but it does have a lasting cost.

On the other hand, if exercising is already a consistent and enjoyable habit for you, then imagining how you'll feel 10 days from now will quickly show you that one skipped workout isn't harmful to your long-term discipline or goals.

And when you're not swayed by this rule or your dilemma of willpower is extra difficult, you can add a final question for yourself. That is, how will breaking willpower now affect you in 10 weeks or even longer-term? You might want to change the parameters to 10 weeks if you're mostly engaged in longer-term decisions and tasks.

In this process, it's crucial to be honest with yourself and wary of your own abilities to rationalize and make excuses. For example, you may have tried to quit an addictive habit many times in the past, only to fail and eventually reinforce the harmful behavior. If you have a history of falling into bad habits after a single lapse in discipline, then an honest assessment of how you would feel after 10 days or 10 weeks will tell you that you simply can't afford a lapse in discipline now if you're going to achieve your long-term goals. It wasn't an exception or justified in that one circumstance—it is a reflection of your character for better or worse.

Without that honesty and ability to see your own rationalizing and excuses for what they are, applying this rule may be a futile exercise.

Rule 6: Just 10 Minutes

The final rule is simple, easy, and powerful.

If you want something negative, harmful, or detrimental to your follow through, wait at least 10 minutes before getting it. It's simple and leaves no room for debate or excuses. When you feel an urge, force yourself to wait for 10 minutes before giving in to whatever the urge is. If you're still craving it after 10 minutes, then have it. Or wait 10 more minutes because you've already done it and survived just fine. Simply by choosing to wait you remove the "immediate" from immediate gratification—building discipline and improving decision-making.

Similarly, if you want to quit something beneficial, wait just 10 more minutes. It's the same thought process applied in a different way. Ten minutes is nothing, so you can wait or continue that long easily. Then, if you do it once, it's easy to repeat, isn't it? In other words, say to yourself "just 10 minutes more of willpower" each time you reach a fork in the road.

Another benefit of this rule is the purposeful escalation of good habits. If you've forced yourself to do something productive for 10 minutes, you might end up doing it for 15 or even 20 minutes more. Next time, your tolerance will build such that you're more immune to temptation and distraction—the following time you might continue for an extra six or seven minutes.

Every time you feel distracted, just exercise willpower for a few minutes longer, and you'll steadily follow through better with each escalation. At some iteration of "just 10 minutes more" you'll reach a point of momentum, and that's often enough to carry you for hours.

Takeaways:

- A manifesto is nothing more than a set of rules to follow every day. We might hate rules, but rules take the guesswork out of our days and give us guidelines to follow. They make matters black and white, which is helpful to following through because there is simply no other choice.
- Rule 1: Are you acting out of laziness? If so, is this a characterization you want about yourself?
- Rule 2: Three major tasks a day, maximum. Differentiate between important tasks, urgent tasks, and simple wasted motion.
- Rule 3: Create daily limitations and requirements for yourself. These keep you within the bounds of what you know you need to do. These are also the building blocks of good habits.
- Rule 4: Sometimes we lose sight of what we want to accomplish. Thus, reaffirm your intentions by stating "I want," "I will," and "I won't" statements.

- Rule 5: Try to look into the future, 10 minutes, hours, and days at a time. Do you like what you see when you consider not following through? Is it worth the benefit to the current self at the expense of the future self? Probably not.
- Rule 6: It's just 10 minutes, right? So if you want to quit, it's just 10 minutes. And if you need to wait, it's just 10 minutes.

Chapter 4: Follow-Through Mindsets

Follow-through is 100% mental. It takes a cognitive effort to follow through on something, especially when you hit discouraging obstacles. Mindsets help with that.

What is a mindset? A mindset is a set way of visualizing and approaching situations and problems. Certain mindsets are all it takes to find the will and motivation necessary to follow through on something.

Gerald is an example of someone with a mindset that impeded with his progress. Gerald had many aspirations to create his own business. He was determined in spirit and relished the idea of one day being a well-known and rich entrepreneur like Steve Jobs. While he knew that success is not just something easy that anyone can grab, he did not realize how sometimes success calls for uncomfortable situations.

When he actually endeavored to start his own business, he ran into a lot of situations that cause him fear. For example, he had to make a monetary investment and it terrified him to think that he may lose his money and never get it back. This fear made Gerald uncomfortable. Another thing he hated was having to conserve his money and cut expenses and luxuries he didn't need to devote more money to his start-up. Living without the luxuries he was used to made him quite uncomfortable as well—so much so that he could not handle it.

Instead of adapting to uncomfortable situations and embracing new things that made him feel scared, Gerald freaked out. He decided that the lifestyle of an entrepreneur was not worth it. He liked the idea but was not prepared for the reality. Finding out that starting up a new business was not all sunshine and rainbows made him give up on it. Instead of starting his dream company and having a shot at becoming the next Steve Jobs, Gerald settled back into the job that he hated simply because it was comfortable to him. He never amounted to much and never reached his dreams as a result.

Gerald's mindset was negative, to say the least. He refused to deal with discomfort or make sacrifices that were mildly unpleasant for his dream career. He preferred what he knew over the unknown, even though what he knew did not satisfy him as much as his dream would have satisfied him. That mindset made him choose to approach the situation from the vantage point that it was all bad and not worth it. He focused on the negative and the discomfort and he refused to work around it.

Gerald may have succeeded at his goal had he held a different mindset. But his collection of poor and inflexible mental habits caused him to approach problems incorrectly, which left him with no hope for success. He let himself fail by approaching problems in the wrong way and eventually giving up.

Had he decided to become comfortable with discomfort, he never would have given up just because the going got tough at one point. He could have adjusted to the discomfort of making sacrifices and embracing unknown scary situations, which would have made him better able to found his business and become an entrepreneur.

Mindset 1: It's Worthwhile

Consider what the Chicago Consortium on School Reform (along with many other educational experts) says motivates students to persevere even when things become difficult at school. Three concepts contribute to student success, which are easily transferable to our adult lives.

The first concept is holding the belief that hard work can and will lead to improvement. No matter how hard things get, it is your efforts that will get you the results you desire, nothing else. Everything else is a byproduct of luck—the hard work itself is a prerequisite. Of course, hard work doesn't overcome everything, but it's an essential component that cannot be skipped.

The second concept is having the confidence that you, and people like you, belong in school and that school is a place where you can thrive. You can apply this to settings outside of school.

The heart of this concept is that you believe in yourself and that you are just as good as anyone else. Basically, you need to believe in your own abilities and trust in your opportunities. Don't create self-limiting beliefs that hold you back, such as thinking that you are not as good as everyone else. This belief is illustrated by feeling that you *also* have valuable input at a business meeting or that you have just as much ability to handle a client as *everyone else* in the office.

The final concept is holding the belief that what you are doing is valuable and relevant to your goals. Why would you stick with doing something if you don't see how it benefits you or helps you reach your goals? That would undermine entire chapters of this book.

Understanding why you do something and how it fits into the big picture of what you are trying to accomplish makes it seem more worthwhile. You won't want to quit an endeavor if you think that it is getting you somewhere. You don't even have to see instant gratification and goal completion to know that you are on the right track. Assigning value and remembering how each thing you do ties into your main goal is very important because it helps you feel that you are doing well just by working.

There is a point to everything you do, so every action you take is valuable. An example of this concept at work would be when you feel that the classes you are taking for your degree are pointless. Remember that they are not pointless, because they are leading to your graduation, which in turn will lead to your dream job in the field of your interest.

These concepts can help you because they lend value and meaning to your work, and they can make you feel like you are making a difference just by following through and executing.

Mindset 2: Comfort with Discomfort

Another critical mindset is believing that your journey to success will become supremely uncomfortable at times, so you need to get comfortable with discomfort. Following through is never comfortable because it asks you to do things that are unfamiliar and new. To be successful and never give up, you need to minimize negative consequences of uncomfortable situations by getting immunized to the sense of discomfort.

Sometimes, you feel the need to avoid something that will lead to success out of discomfort. Maybe you are avoiding extra work because you are fatigued, or you are avoiding talking to new people because it makes you nervous. You are actively shutting out success because you want to avoid being uncomfortable for a little while.

Therefore, overcoming your instinct to avoid things just because they are uncomfortable for you at first is essential. Change is always uncomfortable, but it is key to doing things differently in order to find that magical formula for success. Try doing new things outside of your comfort zone. Do something new, try to learn new skills, talk to new people, and practice new actions that you are bad at until you are good at them. Expose yourself to new situations and things. The unfamiliarity will feel very uncomfortable, but you will not be able to expand your horizons and achieve success any other way.

The more you do things that make you uncomfortable, the more comfortable you become with discomfort. You will find that discomfort is a temporary emotion that leaves with exposure to the situation. The benefits of being uncomfortable far outweigh the mild and fleeting unpleasantness of the sensation. Your mind will come to stop fearing discomfort so much when it realizes that discomfort does not actually hurt you.

Meanwhile, staying comfortable by only doing what you know is a bad idea. It is the recipe for complacency and for staying static. You will not make any changes if you do what you always do.

Don't ever give up on things just because they call for some change and discomfort. Discomfort is merely your fear instinct at play and does not actually hurt you, so getting comfortable with it is a good idea.

You can choose to stay home and not meet new people, or you can choose to go out and make valuable connections that will help you reach your goals. You can choose to never learn a new language, or you can choose to learn it and find a wealth of new business opportunities, such as fun jobs overseas or well-paying jobs in translation. By repeatedly going to language classes and talking to new people, you will become conditioned to the sensation of going out of your comfort zone. Thus, you will become comfortable with being uncomfortable. Then you will stop fearing discomfort and you will open yourself up to some positive changes in your life. Just push yourself consistently every day and try new things to expand the edges of your comfort zone and make your life what you dream about.

Mindset 3: Allow Learning

This mindset entails developing the viewpoint that following through and finishing equals learning and evaluating yourself. You are essentially testing and scoring yourself based on your progress. Giving up is an automatic failure.

When you finish something, on the other hand, you ace the test. You get to see how you do and you get to evaluate your performance. You also gain a lot of valuable skills and information that can help form your success and enable you to try again with better success should you ever fail at something.

You only learn certain things if you see them through to the end. You are in a constant state of seeking information and knowledge, which you can only gain when you complete a project in its entirety. Otherwise, you don't catch the full glimpse of how things work. You get to learn about what it takes to finish something and what you are made of if you follow through. If you don't follow through, then you don't learn all that you have to do and you don't learn anything about yourself except that you are lazy or afraid or a failure.

You can also teach yourself what doesn't work. If you follow through to the end and still don't succeed, you can evaluate your work and see where you went wrong. Then you can avoid that issue in the future. You can become more successful in the future as a result. View life as a series of lessons that you can use for future betterment.

Viewing your endeavors as quests for knowledge can make challenges seem less daunting. It takes the fear out of failing because you still gain knowledge. You will be less inclined to just give up when faced with a challenge because you instead want to learn how to work around the challenge.

You want to see what happens when you try something to overcome the challenge. You will gain no knowledge if you don't follow through, so you have to have the mindset to leap over challenges more fearlessly.

One way to adopt this mindset is to ask yourself, "What can I learn from this?" That breeds a thirst for knowledge, which can be infinitely more motivating than any other mindset. You get curious and you want to see what the finish line looks like. You want to gain the experience that your endeavor can give you, so you go after follow-through in order to get that experience.

Mindset 4: De-Stress

Stress affects how much willpower and self-control you have. You may not be consciously aware, but think about how little you can get done if you're stressed out or anxious. Even more so if you're simply tired and fatigued. Your working spirit is more delicate than you might imagine, which is why it's important to protect it and *de-stress*.

An Australian study showed that students who were stressed because of their exams neglected healthy habits like maintaining a proper diet, getting enough sleep, and exercising. They also smoked more, consumed more caffeine, struggled with controlling their emotions, and paid less attention to household chores, self-care habits, commitments, and spending.

It's easy to conclude the following: if you fail to take care of your mental health, your discipline and willpower quickly deteriorate. Prevent this situation by introducing stress-reducing habits in your life. Each day, spend at least 30 minutes doing relaxing activities. Meet with friends. Read a book. Listen to music. Meditate. Exercise. Cuddle. Take a walk in the woods. Whatever works for you to unwind and turn your brain off.

It's important to relax when you can and overall be aware of your *affect*—the psychological term for the emotions you are feeling and overall temperament.

Why? Because *negative affect* is among the most important triggers of self-control failure. For instance, depressed people desire specific things that bring immediate gratification and procrastinate or avoid any activity that involves effort. Emotional distress causes a behavioral shift toward immediate improvements in mood, and so people make poor decisions. This gets even worse when you realize that *projection bias* occurs every day without our conscious knowledge.

Projection bias is when people falsely project their *current* feelings onto their *future* feelings. If you feel depressed, stressed, and tired, you imagine you'll feel that way next time you want to follow through and finish something. Of course, there's no correlation, but people routinely fail to see that there is no solid connection between these feelings.

For example, people condemn junk food when they aren't hungry without realizing how much they want those delicious cookies once they are hungry. When you plan your diet, you are probably calm and in a mood to make drastic changes. You can also see projection bias as overenthusiasm that your current feelings are how you will feel about something *forever*.

Point being? Don't underestimate the impact of stress on your ability to follow through.

Takeaways:

- Following through is 100% mental, which means it's probably a good idea to talk about the mindsets you attempt to embody.
- Mindset 1: It's all worthwhile. If you feel that your hard work will get you somewhere, you belong and are as good as anyone else, and you feel impact toward your overall goals, execution is easier to stick with.
- Mindset 2: Become comfortable with discomfort. Everything you want to do will have elements of discomfort, unless you just want to watch television all day by yourself. Thus, becoming used to this feeling allows you to tackle what you want without fear.
- Mindset 3: Without following through, there is no learning. Only when you finish something can you evaluate yourself and correct your errors.

Embody an information-gathering mindset.

- Mindset 4: The detrimental power of stress and anxiety can't be overstated. Even being in a poor mood is dangerous to your productivity and follow-through. Be aware and take proactive measures to modulate your stress levels.

Chapter 5: The Science of Smashing Procrastination

Procrastination is a huge problem in following through. How can you approach it effectively?

Madeleine has a big project coming up soon. Her deadline is in a week. She knows that to meet this deadline, she has to complete 15 pages of code a day. But when it comes down to it, she just cannot work. So she puts it off, planning to write 30 the next day to make up for lost progress. Then she can't write 30 pages so she puts it off and now has to write 45. Now she is right on her deadline with almost no code written.

She pulls an all-nighter and sends in a code that is rife with errors. She ran into many challenges with this code that she did not have time to solve because she was so far behind in work. The client rejects the code and is not happy. Madeleine just earned a bad review and no repeat client.

Michelle works on the same types of projects. Unlike Madeleine, Michelle understands what her challenges may be. She breaks the work into small, manageable parts and writes what she can each day and gives herself rewards for every section she completes. Usually she is able to meet or exceed the 15 pages minimum quota that she has set for herself. At the end of the week, she compiles the code with no errors and sends it to her client. He is very happy to have a working code that runs well and he pays her well. She earns a five-star review and the client is eager to hire her again for future projects.

The difference between these two coders is that Michelle succeeded at her project by not procrastinating. She used a system called temptation bundling to ensure that she did not put off work. That gave her plenty of time to not only write code but to find and fix bugs. Madeleine did not use this foresight so she produced poor-quality work. You can see how procrastination leads to intense stress, frustration, and sloppy work.

We all know what procrastination is. But why is such a common issue in people trying to meet deadlines and get quality work done? There are some answers regarding this covered by behavioral psychology.

The main component in this self-defeating habit is called *time inconsistency*. This is where humans value immediate and instant gratification over long-term rewards.

Imagine that you have two selves, a present self and a future self. In this instance, they are completely different people with different desires that do not overlap. When you make goals, you are making plans for your future self. It is easy to plan for what is best for your future self. You can see what you need in the future and you want that so you plan for it. Researchers have found that envisioning your ideal future reality is quite easy.

However, only your present self can actually do anything. To make goals reality, your present self has to take action. Sadly, your present self wants rewards *now.* It does not want to wait to see the results in the future. So it wants to avoid having to do work for long-term goals, favoring instead tasks that reward you right now. For example, you want to get a big project done to make money, but you really need a nap. You are going to choose the nap over work because that's an immediate reward for your present self. Meanwhile, you are hurting your future self by napping instead of working.

Your future self wants goals that pay out at some future date after work performed in the present. The present self wants rewards that pay out now, which in turn often hurt your chances to get your future self its long-term rewards.

The best way to counteract time inconsistency is to move future long-term rewards into the present more effectively. That way, your present self sees the benefit and wants to stick to the long-term program. Waiting for a future reward is often not sufficient to motivate your present self because your present self does not want to wait.

Temptation Bundling

Temptation bundling is an excellent and efficient way to kill procrastination and increase productivity by combining present and future selves and their conflicting needs.

This takes the above concept and introduces the means to reducing temptation to neglect your future self in the present moment. Conceived by behavioral Katy Milkman at the University of Pennsylvania, temptation bundling is a way to blend both future and present self needs by making future rewards more immediate. You give yourself instant gratification in the present while also achieving goals that benefit your future self in the long-term.

It's simpler than it sounds.

Basically, you make a positive (but difficult) behavior or habit in the long-term feel good at the present moment as well. Think eating Twinkies while working out, working out while watching TV, or doing work while soaking your feet in a salt bath—these are examples of ways to make the long-term feel good at the present moment.

There is no need to suffer in the present to get something done for your future self; if you do suffer, then you will lose all motivation and procrastinate. So find ways to bundle your temptations with your long-term goals. In other words, pair your obligations with instantaneous rewards.

Milkman found that up to 51% of her study participants were willing to exercise with temptation bundling. It is an effective means to correct procrastination habits. You should make a list with two columns, one side being your guilty pleasures or temptations and the other side being things you need to do for your future self. Then figure out creative ways to link the two conflicting columns in harmony.

Suppose you like chocolate, surfing, soccer, and running. But work, homework, and piano lessons stand in your way. How might you combine things to make the unpleasurable more tolerable?

Small, Easy Increments

Another way to mitigate procrastination is to start in small, easy increments. Really, you want to break tasks down into minuscule, microscopic components. This makes your first step seem incredibly easy—and taking that first step is the hardest part with procrastination.

Think of procrastination as an enormous wall you must climb. If you collect enough small pebbles and rocks, you can eventually create a step for yourself high enough to simply walk over the wall. You can collect boulders the size of your torso, and you may get the same result, but it's a much tougher road.

Just make sure your barriers to starting are extremely low. For example, you can even complete 95% of a task and leave the remaining 5% as a starter task for later, so you can get back in the swing of things easily. Doing this breaks inertia and enables you to gain forward momentum. You gain momentum by working and creating work that you can build off of later as you tackle the harder parts of the project.

Small and easy increments involve two key parts. The first part is to break your tasks into smaller, more manageable steps. Don't view your task as one huge boulder that you have to get done all at once. Rather, view it as a series of steps to take from Point A to Point B. Your mind will thank you for this as things suddenly seem easier and more doable. An example of this is to view the writing project you have ahead of you as a series of paragraphs only 100 words long.

Maybe you have to write 100 pages, but don't look at it that way. Look it as taking baby steps with short paragraphs. After you complete so many paragraphs, you have written your 100 pages. Small tasks build up rapidly, especially when you are not procrastinating, so create tiny, mentally palatable steps that you can take to build something monumental and reach your ultimate goal. A book is composed of words, after all.

The second part is to start with the easiest tasks first. This may seem counterintuitive. Why would you leave all the hard stuff for later? Remember that procrastination is about making the first step as easy as possible. You are encouraging yourself and proving to your mind that this task is more than possible with each easy task that you tick off your to-do list. By the time you reach the harder tasks, they will seem more attainable and surmountable to your mind since your mind has already done a lot of work.

Inertia is the force that builds as you are at rest. On the other hand, momentum is the drive to keep moving forward until you get everything done. Your task here is to break inertia and gain momentum. Small and easy increments accomplish that because nothing else will get you moving more quickly.

Back to the writing example: consider how you can do the easy parts, such as the outline and the research notes. Write the parts that take the least effort first. Get the bulk of it done, the easy and simple things that are not hard but that take up a lot of time. Leave the hardest 5% of the writing for last for when you have momentum. You will not feel so frustrated and overwhelmed, and thus you will not consider this writing task a huge sacrifice that taxes your present self. You will accomplish it and not suffer, which offers some pleasure to your present self.

Consider Risks

A final tactic is to consider what may go wrong. Being hypervigilant about *what may go wrong* is a tactic employed by highly successful and productive people like Bill Gates. Jim Collins explores this tactic in his book *Great By Choice*. Referring to this as *productive paranoia*, he discusses how people like Bill Gates were constantly paranoid about what may go wrong. By always planning for the worst and trying to avoid the worst, these people actually ended up working extremely hard. They were always focused on their projects just to avoid the worst possible scenarios. As a result, fear motivated them and kept them from procrastination.

Be paranoid and start to question what could go wrong. Think about making contingency plans and working to avoid certain challenges or problems. Thinking about what can go wrong can serve to make you work to avoid things going wrong. As a result, you become more productive just because you are afraid and hypervigilant at the moment.

Be sure to ask yourself how you might lose out if you delay taking action at this moment. The opportunity may go to someone more proactive. Your opportunity may even simply go away, since many things are time-sensitive. Consider how disastrous it could be to your success. The fear of losing out will motivate you. Sure, fear is not a pleasant motivator. But if it works, why not use it? Knowing that you are in danger of some kind kicks you into overdrive. Procrastination comes from boredom, complacency, and safety, so stripping those feelings away can leave you paranoid and eager to avoid bad consequences.

Of course, fear is not a fun motivator, so only use this tactic in small, safe doses. Doing it too much can really drain you and stress you out. As we all know, stress is damaging to your working spirit. Avoid stress and only use this tactic when you begin to feel an intense temptation to procrastinate.

Our opening example of Madeleine could have used fear to help her detect possible mistakes and thus to motivate herself to write her code each day. Using fear, she would have planned to leave plenty of wiggle room in her schedule so that she could properly compile the code and ensure that there were no errors in her code writing. She would have anticipated possible errors and would have worked each day in order to give herself time to catch and fix these errors.

Takeaways:

- Tackling procrastination is similar to pushing Sisyphus's stone. You can beat it back for a bit, but it's so natural that you will never be fully rid of it. The problem is typified by time inconsistency, where we comprise two selves that don't have overlapping desires—one wants gratification in the future and the other wants it right now.
- Temptation bundling is an effective method to battle procrastination. It consists of combining your unpleasurable tasks with something pleasurable. This mainly works because you are battling time inconsistency and

giving both selves what they want simultaneously.

- Start easy and small. Procrastination thrives off inertia. Therefore, you need to make the path to motion and action as easy as possible. Then eventually you can gain momentum—the opposite of inertia.

- Sometimes beating procrastination just requires a kick in the pants. Fear and productive paranoia can do that to you— if you are so fearful of the negative repercussions you will face, then you will certainly be spurred into action. But this is not a method to use very frequently.

Chapter 6. No Distraction Zone

This is a chapter that promises to kick your butt. It's full of powerful techniques to ensure that you jump into action. Without further ado, let's jump into it.

<u>Minimizing Distractions</u>

We often think that distractions can be our friends when it comes to self-discipline. If willpower is finite, then we reason that it's better to take a break, refresh, and distract ourselves from urges and temptations.

Baba Shiv, a professor of marketing at the Stanford Graduate School of Business, conducted a study that illustrates how distractions affect us. Shiv distracted one group of participants by asking them to remember a phone number and then asked all the study participants to choose either chocolate cake or fruit. Those who were trying to remember phone numbers chose the cake 50% more often than those who weren't. The conclusion here is that focus is an essential part of being disciplined.

If you're constantly distracted, you succumb to temptations without even giving yourself a chance to exercise your willpower. It just doesn't occur to you, and you choose the path of least resistance despite your best intentions. Distractions sneakily eat away at our self-discipline. This process can go on in the background so that we don't even realize that our discipline is lapsing until it's too late and all of our past efforts have been wasted.

The design of checkout lanes in supermarkets is a prime example of capitalizing on distracted minds and depleted willpower. You can make healthy decisions every step of the way through the grocery store, but you can't escape without one final distraction of candy, chocolate, and snacks at the register. This is frequently the most difficult time to be disciplined because you're so close to exiting and thinking ahead and the items are cheap and available to purchase instantly.

What should you do with this knowledge? If you work in a cluttered environment, clean it up. A clean desk can help create a clear mind, and a clear mind is much more able to remain disciplined. A Cornell University study provides some compelling evidence supporting the concept of *"out of sight, out of mind"* as a means of improving discipline, and it applies to far more beyond your desk.

The study participants were given a jar full of Hershey's Kisses that was either clear or opaque and either placed on their desk or six feet away. On average, the participants ate 7.7 Kisses per day from the clear jars on their desks as opposed to 4.6 per day from opaque jars in the same location. When the jars were placed six feet away, the participants ate 5.6 Kisses per day from the clear jars and 3.1 per day from the opaque jars.

Surprisingly, the study subjects consistently reported feeling that they had eaten more Kisses when the jars were placed six feet away, even though the opposite was true. That discrepancy is a crucial piece of information because it provides a simple guideline for improving discipline. That is, you can use laziness to your advantage by clearing your workplace of distractions. You may not completely forget about those distractions, but the more effort it takes for you to give in to a temptation, the less likely you are to do so. Furthermore, it eliminates some of the most counterproductive discipline lapses—the mindless ones that we don't even realize we are doing.

It's so much easier to reach your hand into a cookie jar without thinking about it if that jar is easily accessible and visible. Those are the types of scenarios that you want to avoid when designing an environment for discipline. If you place the cookie jar in a distant cabinet, you don't eliminate the temptation altogether but you make it so that giving in to the temptation requires a lot of effort. That makes a big difference.

Ultimately, you want to create an environment for yourself that is clear of distractions and obvious temptations. You can make discipline drastically easier just by eliminating the mindless and effortless lapses in discipline that are made possible by an environment that hasn't been optimized. This applies to your desk, your workspace, your office, what you can see from your desk, and even your computer desktop. Keep them clear of distractions as much as possible and you'll simply forget about them. In your lapses of discipline or boredom, you'll have no other option than to keep working.

Default to Positive Actions and Behaviors

Optimizing your environment for self-discipline really comes down to understanding how automatic most of your decision-making is.

To illustrate that point, consider the findings of a study conducted in 11 European countries on organ donors. The data showed that countries that automatically have citizens opted-in to being organ donors—requiring action to opt-out—had rates at or above 95% participation. When the default choice was not to be an organ donor, however, the highest rate found in any of the 11 countries was a mere 27% participation. Ultimately, people just went with the option that required the least effort. It said nothing about their actual intention or desire to be an organ donor.

This same concept of defaulting to the more desirable choice can be applied to your own self-discipline. We're lazy and will happily accept whatever is in front of our faces. You can make it easy for yourself to choose whichever options most benefit you while also making it as difficult as possible to make harmful decisions.

A default option is one that the decision-maker chooses if he or she does nothing or the minimal amount of effort. In other contexts, default options also include those that are normative or suggested. Countless experiments and observational studies have shown that making an option the default will increase the likelihood of it being chosen, which is known as the default effect. Making decisions requires energy, so we often choose the default option to conserve energy and avoid making decisions, especially when we aren't familiar with what it is we are making a decision about.

Optimizing these default decisions is where the bulk of your efforts to make a more discipline-conducive environment can take place. You might believe that you control the majority of your choices, but in reality, that isn't the case. Instead, a significant amount of your actions are just responses to your environment.

If you're distracted by social media, for example, you might move the app icons to the back page of your phone so that you aren't constantly seeing them whenever you open your phone to do something else. Better yet, you can log out of the apps after each use or delete them from your phone altogether so that you'll only use them when you really want to instead of letting them be distractions.

And if you're in the habit of mindlessly picking up your phone while working, you can simply start placing it faced down and far enough away that you have to get up to reach it. If you want to practice violin more, put it on your desk with your music notes open. If you want to floss your teeth more, keep floss in your backpack, in your bathroom, on your nightstand, and on your sofa.

There is a seemingly endless number of examples of how you can utilize the default effect to become more disciplined with very little use of willpower itself. Another one is that leaving potato chips and cookies out on the kitchen counter will make it your default choice to eat those things whenever you walk to the kitchen feeling even the slightest bit hungry. Hiding those (or not buying them at all) and replacing those unhealthy snacks with fruit will instantly increase the probability that you eat fruit and that you avoid the unhealthy snacks. Want to exercise more? Put a pull-up bar in your bathroom doorway.

If you keep sugary sodas and juices in your refrigerator, you're making it your default choice to drink them whenever you are thirsty and open the fridge. But if you don't have those options, you increase the likelihood that you'll drink water or make tea. Want to take more vitamins? Put them right next to your toothbrush for easier access.

If you sit in an office all day and have back problems, then you might benefit from standing up and walking frequently throughout the day. You can make this your default option by drinking water constantly so that you are forced to get up to go to the bathroom. Or perhaps you could schedule alarms on your phone and place it somewhere out of reach so that you have to stand up to turn off the alarm whenever it goes off.

The whole point of this is that you can save your willpower and your energy by making positive changes to your environment. The two biggest facets of environmental change are reducing clutter and distractions and optimizing choices based on the default effect.

If you reduce distractions from your environment, you'll clear your mind, which in turn increases focus, efficiency, and productivity. Furthermore, you can use your dopamine reward system to your advantage by reinforcing your own good habits while also cutting back on mindless pursuits of small pleasures. Finally, you can make it so the path with the least effort leads to the choices you desire and benefit from.

These all make it so you can sidestep actually using discipline and to save it for your bigger daily challenges. After all, why exercise willpower when you don't need to if you can plan around it?

Attention Residue

Sometimes focusing on work can be difficult, and you find yourself wondering just why it's so hard to stay on track and ignore shiny objects. Luckily, there is an explanation for this. In 2009, Sophie Leroy published a paper that was aptly titled "Why Is It So Hard to Do My Work?" In it, she explained an effect that she called attention residue.

Leroy noted that other researchers had studied the effect of multitasking on performance but that in the modern work environment, once you reached a high enough level, it was more common to find people working on multiple projects sequentially. "Going from one meeting to the next, starting to work on one project and soon after having to transition to another is just part of life in organizations," Leroy explains.

This is essentially the modern version of multitasking—working on projects in short bursts and switching between them, not necessarily doing them all at once. People may not actually be working on multiple tasks at the same time, but it's nearly as bad to keep switching between them in relatively quick succession. For all intents and purposes, this is multitasking.

The problem identified by this research is that you cannot switch seamlessly between tasks without a delay of sorts. When you switch from Task A to Task B, your attention doesn't immediately follow—a residue of your attention remains stuck thinking about the original task. This becomes worse and the residue becomes especially "thick" if your work on Task A was unbounded and of low intensity before you switched, but even if you finish Task A before moving on, your attention remains divided for a while.

Leroy's tests forced people to switch between different tasks in a laboratory setting. In one of these experiments, she started the subjects working on a set of word puzzles. In one of the trials, she would interrupt their work and force them to move on to a new and challenging task—for example, reading resumes and making hypothetical hiring decisions. In other trials, she let the subjects finish the puzzles before giving them the next task.

While the participants were switching between puzzling and hiring, Leroy would play a quick lexical decision game. This was so she could quantify the amount of leftover residue from the first task. The results were clear: "People experiencing attention residue after switching tasks are likely to demonstrate poor performance on that next task," and the more intense the residue, the worse the performance.

This doesn't seem too far of a stretch when you think about it. We've all experienced that frantic moment when we're doing too many things at once and suddenly find ourselves unable to do any at all. How can you concentrate on any task if you keep switching back and forth between two or more different things? You'll likely be stuck simply trying to make sense of everything and organize it so you can understand it. It will only force you to waste time trying to catch up to where you were instead of pushing forward. You'll take one step forward but two steps back each time you try.

Even worse news is presented by a Stanford researcher, Clifford Nass, who examined the work pattern of people who multitask. The researchers split their subjects into two groups: those who regularly do a lot of media multitasking and those who don't. In one experiment, the groups were shown sets of two red rectangles alone or surrounded by two, four, or six blue rectangles. Each configuration was flashed twice, and the participants had to determine whether the two red rectangles in the second frame differed from the first.

It sounds simple enough: just ignore the blue rectangles and see if the red ones change. In fact, it was quite simple, and those who didn't often multitask had no trouble doing this. However, the high multitaskers performed terribly as they were constantly distracted by the irrelevant blue images.

Because they couldn't ignore the images, the researchers thought that maybe they were better at storing and organizing information. Maybe they had better memories. But this was proven wrong by the second test. After being shown sequences of alphabetical letters, the high multitaskers also struggled to remember when a letter was making a repeat appearance. And again, the low multitaskers performed better overall. It was as simple as that.

"The low multitaskers did great," Ophir said. "The high multitaskers were doing worse and worse the further they went along because they kept seeing more letters and had difficulty keeping them sorted in their brains."

Multitasking may seem to be the best of both worlds, but when you're in situations where there are multiple sources of information coming from the external world or emerging from memory, you cannot filter out what is irrelevant to your current goal. This failure to filter means that you are slowed down by irrelevant information and will struggle to complete a task without distractions. It is much easier to focus on one thing at once, without letting distractions interfere, than to try doing several things at a time and overload your brain with too much information.

From both of these experiments, it's clear that multitasking isn't really good for anything, and all attempts to do it don't really lead anywhere. By multitasking you are neither able to adequately focus on each new task nor able to ignore any distractions that are hindering your work. There might be certain ways you can multitask 1% more effectively, but the overall lesson is just to avoid it whenever possible.

Singletasking. What does this mean?

To set everything else aside and not check, monitor, email, or even touch anything other than the current task you are working on. It requires singular focus and the purposeful and intentional tuning out of everything else. Switch off your notifications and ditch your phone. If you must be on your computer, keep only one browser tab or program open at a time. A lot of singletasking is about consciously avoiding distractions that seem small and harmless. The biggest culprits? Your electronic devices. Ignore them when possible.

Keep a spotless workspace so your eye doesn't catch something that needs cleaning or adjusting. Ideally, singletasking reduces your environment to a blank room because you shouldn't pay attention to any of it.

Attempt to pay attention to when you are being interrupted or subtly switching between tasks. This is hard to catch at first and will require you to make conscious decisions against your instincts.

Something that will be very hard to resist is to tell yourself that you must act on something immediately and interrupt your task. This is rarely the truth. To combat this urge, set aside a Post-it to take notes for ideas that will inevitably spring to mind regarding other tasks. Just jot them down quickly and return to your primary goal. You can address them after your singletasking period is over, and you won't have forgotten anything. It will keep your mind focused on one single task while setting you up for future success.

Batching

Henry Ford, founder of Ford Motor Company, got a lot of things right about cars.

He had a few competitors back in the day, but a primary reason those names are essentially lost in time is because he was also the creator of the *factory assembly line*. On a factory assembly line, workers focus on one task at a time.

This streamlines a process and makes it far more efficient than having a single worker see a project through from start to finish, switching between multiple tasks. It allows workers to specialize and perfect their task, which cuts down on errors and makes troubleshooting far easier. Workers didn't have to do more thinking than was necessary for the task at hand. For Ford, this made his automobile production efficiency and output shoot through the roof and dominate his market.

That, in essence, is what *batching* can do for you.

Batching is when you group similar tasks together to complete them all at once. Ford's assembly line was essentially 100% batching because his workers only performed one task incredibly efficiently.

Let's take a common example we can all relate to—checking email.

If you have any sort of online presence or job, you probably have a steady stream of emails trickling (or gushing) into your inbox every hour. Constantly checking your email is an extremely inefficient use of time. It interrupts other tasks and scatters your focus whenever you receive a new email. Many of us drop what we're doing to take care of something from an email. Then we have to start the original task over again because our flow and momentum has been interrupted.

Batching emails will considerably improve your productivity. An example of this would be to only check your emails at the top of every two hours and purposely ignore or block your inbox notifications. At first it might be difficult, but limiting how often you check email in this way allows you to focus on your tasks without constantly being distracted and having to re-acclimatize yourself.

Perhaps more importantly, it teaches the lesson that saying no to some tasks is just as important as saying yes to the correct ones. Batching teaches the art of purposeful, deliberate ignorance so you can focus on other tasks.

Switching from task to task is a large mental burden because you are essentially stopping and starting from zero numerous times throughout the day. It takes a lot of energy to switch from task to task, and there are usually a few wasted minutes just regaining your bearings and figuring out the status of the task you were working on. Of course, these kinds of interruptions only lead to achieving just a portion of what you can and want to.

In the example of checking email, batching allows you to stay in a mindset of reading and composing email with all its associated skills, tasks, and reminders. Email is a distinctly different mindset and way of thinking than designing a new graphic for an advertising campaign. Staying in the same mindset pays huge dividends.

Batching allows you to save your mental energy for the tasks themselves and not waste your energy on the process of switching back and forth between them.

What else can you batch? You can schedule all your meetings in one afternoon so you will have a free, uninterrupted morning to work. You can plan to do everything that requires computer access in the morning and even batch parts of tasks such as the parts that require you to make phone calls.

You can also batch your distractions. This isn't to distract and amuse yourself more efficiently; it's to make sure that you are conserving your energy and allowing your focused time to be exactly that—focused.

How can you batch distractions? For example, if you're burned out on a particular task, you might want to take a little social media break. By all means, take it! However, allot just a bit more time to check *all* of your accounts: ESPN, Refinery29, and whatever other distractions you occupy yourself with. Grab a new cup of coffee, take a brisk walk around the office, and say hello to your neighbor.

Get it all out of your system so that when you're back to work, you can have a solid and fixed block of time in which to focus. After all, if there is nothing new on your Facebook page, you will probably feel less compelled to check it. Once you knock yourself out doing all these distracting activities within the allotted time, you can switch to productive work for the rest of your hour.

The more you divide your attention among different activities, the less productive you'll be. However, if you begin doing something similar to the previous activity, you'll find it's much easier to get going because your mind is already geared toward doing a certain kind of task. Do all the similar tasks together, one after the other, and then move on to the next batch of similar or related activities. Effective batching can skyrocket your productivity no matter the context.

"Don't-Do" List

Everyone knows the value of the to-do list— no doubt you've stumbled across tips elsewhere about using a to-do list to increase productivity.

But everyone inherently *kind of* knows what they should be doing and when they need to do it by. The act of writing it down just helps remind them, and it makes people more likely to take care of their obligations.

However, not everyone knows what they *shouldn't* be doing—what they should be avoiding, common ways of procrastinating, and distractions that masquerade as priorities. Along with your to-do list, it's equally important to make a *don't-do list*. Each day, we're faced with choosing tasks that will create the biggest impact for us, and there are many hidden obstacles.

Again, we all know the obvious evils to avoid when trying to upgrade productivity: social media, goofing around on the Internet, watching *The Bachelorette* while trying to work, and learning to play the flute while reading.

It can be difficult to distinguish between real tasks and useless tasks, and it will require some hard thought on your part.

You need to fill your don't-do list with tasks that will sneakily steal your time and undermine your goals. These are tasks that are insignificant or a poor use of your time, tasks that don't help your bottom line, and tasks that have a serious case of diminishing returns the more you work on them.

If you continuously devote and waste your time on these tasks, your real priorities and goals will be left untouched. Here's what you should put on your *don't*-do list.

First, include tasks that are priorities but which you can't do anything about at present because of external circumstances.

These are tasks that are important in one or many ways but are waiting for feedback from others or for underlying tasks to be completed first. Put these on your don't-do list because there is literally nothing you can do about them!

Don't spend your mental energy thinking about them. They'll still be there when you hear back from those other people. Just note that you are waiting to hear back from someone else and note the date on which you need to follow-up if you haven't heard back. Then push these out of your mind because they're on someone else's to-do list, not yours. You can also temporarily push things off your plate by clarifying and asking questions of other people. This puts the ball in their court to act, and you can take that time to catch up on other matters.

Second, include tasks that don't add value as far as your projects are concerned.

There are many small items that don't add to your bottom line, and often these are trivial things—busy work. Can you delegate these, assign them to someone else, or even outsource them? Do they really require your time? In other words, are they *worth* your time? And will anyone but you notice the difference if you delegate the task to someone else? By taking on the task yourself, are you getting stuck in the weeds of perfectionism? You should spend your time on big tasks that move entire projects forward and not myopic, trivial tasks. Often these are useless tasks disguised as important ones, such as selecting the paint color for the bike shed in the parking lot of the nuclear power plant you are building.

Third, include tasks that are current and ongoing but will not benefit from additional work or attention paid to them.

These tasks suffer from diminishing returns. These tasks are just a waste of energy because while they can still stand to improve (and is there anything that can't?), the amount of likely improvement will either not make a difference in the overall outcome or success or will take a disproportionate amount of time and effort without making a significant dent.

For all intents and purposes, these tasks should be considered *done*. Don't waste your time on them, and don't fall into the trap of considering them a priority. Once you finish everything else on your plate, you can then evaluate how much time you want to devote to polishing something.

If the task is at 90% of the quality you need it to be, it's time to look around at what else needs your attention to bring it from 0% to 90%. In other words, it's far more helpful to have three tasks completed at 80% quality versus one task at 100% quality.

When you consciously avoid the items on your don't-do list, you keep yourself focused and streamlined. You don't waste energy or time, and your daily output will increase dramatically.

Why read a menu with food items that are unavailable? It's pointless and wastes your mental bandwidth. By preventing your energy level from being dissipated by those things that suck up your time and attention, a don't-do list enables you to focus on what matters.

This can have a very dramatic and positive impact on your daily routine. The fewer things that tug on your mind, the better—the kind of stress and anxiety they create only hampers or kills productivity. A don't-do list will free your mind from the burden of having too many things in the air because it eliminates most of those things! You can focus on the balls that are still in flight and steadily knock each one out.

The 40–70 Rule

Many of us are reluctant to take actions outside the comfort zone unless we have all the pertinent information we need. But can you actually have *too* much information to start something new?

Former U.S. Secretary of State Colin Powell has a rule of thumb about making decisions and coming to a point of action. He says that any time you face a hard choice, you should have *no less* than 40% and *no more* than 70% of the information you need to make that decision. In that range, you have enough information to make an informed choice but not so much intelligence that you lose your resolve and simply stay abreast of the situation.

If you have less than 40% of the information you need, you're essentially shooting from the hip. You don't know quite enough to move forward and will probably make a lot of mistakes. Conversely, if you chase down more data until you get more than 70% of what you need (and it's unlikely that you'll truly need anything above this level), you could get overwhelmed and uncertain. The opportunity may have passed you by and someone else may have beaten you by starting already.

But in that sweet spot between 40% and 70%, you have enough to go on and let your intuition guide your decisions. In the context of Colin Powell, this is where effective leaders are made: the ones who have instincts that point in the right direction are who will lead their organization to success.

For our purposes of breaking out of the comfort zone, we can replace the word "information" with other motivators: 40–70% of experience, 40–70% reading or learning, 40–70% confidence, or 40–70% of planning. While we're completing the task, we'll also be doing analyzing and planning on the fly, so this range of certainty helps us tend toward action.

When you try to achieve more than 70% information (or confidence, experience, etc.), your lack of speed can result in many negative consequences. It can also destroy your momentum or stem your interest, effectively meaning nothing's going to happen. There is a high likelihood of gaining nothing further from surpassing this threshold.

For example, let's say you're opening up a cocktail bar, which involves buying a lot of different types of liquor. You can't expect to have absolutely all the liquor you will ever need ready when the doors are ready to open. But on the other hand, it doesn't make sense to commence operations without enough for customers to choose from.

So you'd wait until you have at least 40% of available inventory. You've got momentum established. You figure if you could get more than half of what you need, you'll be in pretty good shape to open. You might not be able to make absolutely every drink in the bartender's guide, but you'll have enough on-hand to cover the staple drinks with a couple of variations. If you have around 50–60% inventory, you're probably ready. When the remaining inventory arrives, you'll already be in action and can just incorporate that new inventory into your offerings. If you waited until you had 70% or more inventory, you could find yourself stuck in neutral for longer than you wanted to be.

This way of thinking leads to more action than not. Waiting until you have 40% of what you need to make a move isn't a sedentary stay inside your comfort zone—you're actively planning what you need to do to get out, which is just fine (as long as it's not overplanning). Making the execution before you're 100%—or even halfway—ready to do so is the kind of gutsy move that shakes you out of the indifference of your comfort zone in a hurry.

Do Nothing

Burn-out is a very real risk, especially in today's modern age where to get ahead, it seems that everyone has a full-time job as well as a side career that is aimed toward making money. We seek to intentionally pack our days full of activities, professional and social, as a means of squeezing the last drop of enjoyment out of our lives.

Ironically, this quickly becomes counterproductive because very few people have a battery that can function like that. As for what that means for your brain, any shred of fatigue will affect your clarity of thought. That part should be clear from our own lives. We function better on eight hours of sleep versus three hours of sleep.

However, what's less obvious is that disconnecting from everything and doing nothing at all can actually be a path to greater creativity and insight. There's a reason that when we are zoning out at the gym or in the shower, we seem to have a disproportionate number of epiphanies. Thought is inherently fatiguing and taxing on the mind and is characterized by the brain emitting beta waves. Relaxation and a lack of attention, on the other hand, is characterized by the brain emitting alpha waves.

What are alpha waves also associated with? Studies by Professor Flavio Frohlich, among others, have shown that alpha waves are associated with enhanced memory, creative thinking, and overall increased happiness.

Maybe that's the reason meditation and practicing mindfulness is being pushed so hard these days. They intentionally slow you down and put you into a state of releasing alpha waves, which trigger increased happiness and life satisfaction. Most of the world's top performers, such as CEOs, always mention meditation as a vital part of their daily routine—this is likely why. The ability to tune things out allows them to function at their peak when it matters, like a battery recharge in the middle of the day.

For the high achievers out there, it's not necessarily a matter of taking a break just to generate some alpha waves. Don't think of it as rest; think of it as recovering so you can get ready when you need to really think creatively.

We instinctively know to sleep, stretch, and warm up our bodies if we have an athletic competition, but we disregard doing the same for our minds. When you relax more and do nothing at all, you enter a state of allowing your mind to wander, and you also come back recharged and refreshed.

Allow yourself to daydream because when was the last time your daydreams were boring and routine versus creative and outlandish? If you need a break, resist the urge to pick up your phone and scroll through your social media. Just staring into blank space might be a better use of your time!

Takeaways:

- Minimize your distractions in your environment. It turns out that out of sight is out of mind with distractions, so don't keep anything stimulating near your workstation otherwise your willpower will slowly deplete itself.
- Create default actions wherever possible. This is where the easiest and lowest resistance past for you is the path you want the most. This is also done through curating and designing your environment for productivity.

- Singletasking is an important concept because it definitively proves the flaws of multitasking. When you switch from task to task, you create attention residue. This means it takes a while for you to adjust to each new task, even if you were already familiar with it. You can eliminate this by singletasking, and also by batching, which is when you do all similar types of tasks together to capitalize on your mental efficiency.

- A don't-do list can be just as powerful as a to-do list because we are rarely told what to ignore. As a result, these distractions or sneaky time-suckers can invade our space without us even knowing we are being duped. Include tasks you can't move forward on, make progress on, or help.

- The 40–70 rule is when you beat inaction through the amount of information you seek. If you have less than 40%, don't act. But if you have 70%, you must act. You'll never have 100%, and chances are, 70% is more than sufficient—the rest you learn along the way, anyway.

- Finally, you might want to do nothing from time to time. This is rest and relaxation—but you should think of it as mental recovery. What does an athlete do between races or matches? You got it—they recover so they are primed to work again when necessary.

Chapter 7: Deadly Pitfalls

In the science of following through, there are a massive number of mistakes that you could make that could cost you your progress.

Take Michael. Michael is only human. Thus, he made some mistakes with follow-through when he first started his at-home freelance consulting firm. He believed that starting his business would change his life overnight. He imagined getting tons of money for minimal work, having plenty of time to play with his newborn daughter, and even having time to hit the gym and get pumped like Arnold. He imagined that having no boss would free up a lot of his time.

Weeks went by and he did none of those things. In fact, his expectations felt so extreme that they were intimidating and discouraging.

This is called *false hope syndrome*. Michael thought he would accomplish a lot more than was humanly possible. His other mistake was not getting to know himself or how he worked best. He tried to impose an unrealistic schedule on himself that just did not fit his natural circadian rhythm and work preferences.

False hope syndrome occurs when you think that you can do everything on your to-do list and reach your dreams in a short amount of time. You promise yourself, or a client, the moon. Then you are sorely disappointed when you cannot deliver, and those big expectations have actually caused a negative effect on your working spirit. They'll cause you to shrink back and be more fearful of the failure you just experienced, and you may end up in a worse state than you were to begin with.

Michael was extremely disappointed by the lack of huge life changes he saw when he started his business. His life did not change magically overnight. He did not have the energy for all of these changes he was planning to make. Plus, he hated working because he was following the wrong schedule. He began to fall behind on work and procrastinate to avoid the tasks he hated. He tried to work in the morning while drinking three cups of coffee and found he just could not function.

After a while, Michael decided to take a good long look at what he was trying to do and how he was failing. He adjusted his schedule to fit his lifestyle better and stopped working so early in the morning after staying up late with his daughter, who had not yet achieved a normal sleep cycle. He found how to work on only a few goals at a time and make time for his goals when he could.

Suddenly, Michael felt better and worked better. Life was just easier since he fell into a more comfortable and realistic groove. He was no longer so overwhelmed and disappointed, so he stopped despising work and stopped putting work off out of loathing and dread.

Like Michael, we all make mistakes. But learning which mistakes to avoid gives you a step up on other people. You will not tax your self-discipline or willpower for follow-through if you avoid these common mistakes.

False Hope Syndrome

False hope syndrome, what Michael had, is where you overestimate the changes you can make. You set unrealistic expectations for what you can do and the speed, number, and ease of the changes you plan to make to your life. When you can't accomplish everything on your list of desired changes, the disappointment at failing to reach your lofty goals can cause a powerful backlash that will cause you to give up hope.

Even if you have extremely strong self-discipline and desire to change, you will still fail if your expectations are too high. Plan for proper expectations and figure out what you can actually hope for. Learn to let go of hopes that are not realistic and to set expectations that you can actually obtain or meet.

One example of this might be thinking that you will magically be able to change your work habits, even though you have tried doing the same things in the past and have failed. You expect to get more done with distractions and multitasking, for example, even though that has never worked for you before. Changing your approach and not believing that you can initiate too much self-change is essential to being successful because it prevents you from falling into old habits and disappointing yourself.

False hope is about controlling your expectations. When you can have realistic hopes, you can actually achieve, which leads to confidence, competence, and skill. Anything else is just setting yourself up for heartbreak and failure, which tends to not be productive. Don't shoot too high, but don't shoot too low; otherwise, you'll grow bored and unengaged. Just remember that your goals can be entirely different from your expectations.

Overthinking

Another mistake is *overthinking*. Overthinking is a silent killer of joy, hope, and reason. It kills your positivity and desire to carry on. Overthinking makes you inevitably fixate on the negative because they are so easy to find, and your entire worldview eventually goes dark.

Overthinking is so tempting because it mimics progress. After all, you are thinking about work and doing research to make the best decision. You think you are being proactive. But really, overthinking is silently hampering you and this another classic instance of mere motion versus actual action.

You are considering too many options and doing too much research, which limits your ability to make an executive decision. You are wasting time doing research and forming plans for things that don't really matter instead of putting one foot in front of the other and eliminating your inertia.

By overthinking, you freeze your ability to make decisions. Psychologist Barry Schwartz suggests that a *paradox of choice* is harmful because it leads to analysis paralysis. His studies reveal that having more choices actually causes people to develop anxiety and avoid making a choice in the long run. Having fewer present choices helps people narrow it down.

Consider when you go to Walmart and you are faced with buying a new printer for your office. Standing before the wall of printers, all of which have great advertising and boast so many features, you find yourself overwhelmed and can't settle on a printer. You panic and buy the first one you see. (Or you go home without buying one even though you needed it.)

You wasted so much time deliberating over printers and you ended up not even using the information you gained because you got overwhelmed. You can't decide because there is too much information overloading your brain in the process. This is a perfect illustration of how overthinking kills your ability to follow through and execute.

So instead of overthinking, place an emphasis on action. Most actions are reversible—you can easily return a printer to Walmart. But you'll have gained no further information if you stay in the same place without moving.

You can also limit the choices you give yourself and the criterion you use. Focus on the main things you need, and find the easiest choice that meets your needs. Don't fall down the rabbit hole of researching obsessively on Google or comparing thousands of brands to find the best one. Chances are, 90% of them do exactly what you want with little variance. So what are you really deliberating over?

If you are tasked with buying the new office printer, determine three traits your office needs in a printer. Then go to Walmart and buy the cheapest one that meets all of those needs. Put blinders on such that nothing else matters. This is a classic example of limiting your information intake and being willfully ignorant. Overthinking can sneak in because we don't have clarity on what matters, so when you can articulate those, suddenly you can see clear choices.

Worry

Worry is closely related to overthinking and it is the third powerful mistake you might make in following through.

Worrying is when you ruminate on problems, real or imagined. This takes you out of the present, which you have control over, and puts you into the future or past, which you have zero control over.

Worrying steals your control and composure, but taking action and focusing on the present empowers you by letting you get things done now. Try to switch your mindset toward action and solutions rather than problems and mistakes. Furthermore, worrying makes you focus on things that

161

may not even be real and that you cannot change, and you devote time and energy to these worries that you could be spending on work instead.

It's a tall task to tell someone to worry less. But the truth is, worrying causes you to suffer twice—once during the worrying and again if the dreaded event actually occurs. And if it doesn't occur, you've just suffered for no reason at all.

Worrying can also masquerade as productivity, but again, it is wasted motion. It's a lot of energy spent to get nowhere. Focus on what you can control and do something about. Focus on things that are real and have happened, not imaginary outcomes or scenarios that may never come to pass. Do what you can do at the moment, because that's all you can control; in doing so, carry a mindset of action and control rather than fear.

Know Thyself

The final major mistake many people make is failing to get to know themselves.

Knowing yourself enables you to figure out how to work best and create the most beneficial environments for yourself.

Not all people work the same way. One man might like a detailed schedule that lays out every part of his day, while another man needs breathing room and spontaneity. One woman may need a quiet environment where she can work alone while another woman needs friends and a social work environment to thrive in.

Like Michael found out, don't impose unrealistic or unsuitable schedules, ideals, or environments on yourself and expect to succeed. Find what is best for you and then implement that to thrive. You can only work best if you are in your best environment. Find what that environment is instead of forcing yourself to conform to something that does not suit you and instead makes you miserable and hinders your productivity.

When you use your preferences and strengths to your advantage, you are more likely to follow through. This is because you are allowing yourself to work at your best, at your very peak. You're not fighting yourself and are instead working within your flow and accessing your strengths. You are not making yourself miserable by following someone else's formula for success.

Stop judging yourself and others for being different. We are all different. Our productivity is very fragile and requires particular care to flourish. Treat yourself to what helps you thrive if you want to follow through.

Figure out what times you work best during the day. Then work during those times. Don't let others judge you for not being functional before 8:00 a.m. or for working late into the night. Working at your best time will enable you to be more productive and follow through more easily because you are using your energy when you have the most of it. Don't try to work early in the morning if you are not a morning person because that will only lead you to failure.

There is another component to getting to know yourself: diagnosing why you are failing and fixing the underlying problem. It is diagnosing the cause and source of your lack of follow-through so that you can address it. Only when you determine the cause of your poor follow-through can you actually do something about it. Don't make the common mistake of attributing failure to the wrong cause, or you will never be able to address and correct the issue.

Be Sherlock Holmes if you are having trouble with follow-through. Using the power of deduction, deduce what is wrong and why you are not being productive. Maybe you are reading another time management book when you should be keeping a calendar and not wasting time on books. Maybe you are trying to organize and label everything when really you just have too much stuff and need to get rid of some of it. Maybe you are discouraged so you procrastinate and thus keep failing and wondering why your discouragement is growing.

Really consider how you feel when you don't follow through. Look at your feelings during the commencement stage of a project and see if you feel overwhelmed or put things off for too long to reasonably finish them. Why do *you* specifically give up? When you find the reason, you can figure out how to apply one of the rules or mindsets in this book to rectify the problem.

Failure happens, and it's going to happen. It's not the end of the world. It's certainly not the end of productivity. But failure is useful only when we're aware of the cause. When we see the cause, we can see how to fix it and how to avoid repeated failure in the future. When we don't, we're doomed to repeat our mistakes until we do realize what's actually going on. Avoid wasted time by diagnosing your reasons for failure early on.

Takeaways:

- Pitfalls to following through and finishing what you start? Too many to name. But a select few in this chapter are stronger and more dangerous than most.

- False hope syndrome is when you expect that you will be able to change or improve to an unrealistic degree. When you inevitably fail to meet this mark, there is a very real backlash that results in you being even less motivated and disciplined than before you started. To beat this, set proper expectations based on your history and understand the difference between goals and expectations.
- Overthinking is sneaky because it feels like action and it even feels productive. But it's not. Overthinking is when you fixate and can't seem to take the first step toward action. Zero in on the details that matter, deliberately ignore everything else, and you'll feel much more clarity.
- Worrying is when you fixate on something and inevitably start drawing out the negative scenarios and pitfalls. However, worrying is also when you fixate on things you can't control while ignoring what you can control—the present. The solution is to focus on what you can do right now and only right now.

- Do you know yourself? Well, what about in terms of productivity and how you work and produce the best? You can consider time of day, environment, setting, and so on. But you should consider that knowing yourself is also the ability to look at yourself and understand why you may have failed or come up short. It is the ability to self-diagnose and be self-aware.

Chapter 8. Daily Systems for Success

Ned started his own software consulting firm. He was thrilled to be his own boss and did not anticipate that he would have any trouble managing clients, answering emails, generating leads, sending out invoices, performing his consulting work, and so on!

At first, everything in Ned's business was great. He would wake up early, answer emails, and send out newsletters to generate leads. Then he would get to his normal job. When he had spare time, he would get back to emails. Late into the night, he would be working, trying to market himself while also working on his various projects.

But as his business took off, suddenly his inbox was inundated! His list of projects grew longer and longer. Suddenly, he was completely overwhelmed. Putting in 12-hour days at the very least, he struggled to catch up with emails, follow up with clients, send out invoices in a timely manner, and meet deadlines. He felt as if he were drowning. Angry clients would harass him, demanding to know where their work was!

Seeing his desk would have made Martha Stewart weep. Ned would spend up to 15 minutes looking for important papers or notes that he had made on projects. His home office was a jumbled mess. The room that he has so cheerfully painted and decorated was now a prison, where he spent almost all of his time.

Ned himself looked even worse. He looked like a zombie and subsisted on coffee and fast food. His eyes developed deep bags under them.

Then he realized that he was losing leads and losing money. Bad reviews began to pile up on his website and his freelancing profile. It looked as if his consulting firm was failing.

What did Ned do wrong? He didn't use a system. He relied on himself to get everything done and did not implement a way to organize and streamline his work to make it easier. He took on too much at once, trying to accomplish tons of goals each day without using a system to make those goals easier.

Willpower is great to a degree. You certainly need it in your life to push you to be the best that you can be. But relying on your willpower and self-discipline alone to be successful can fail you if you rely on it too heavily because you cannot push yourself past your maximum. Once you hit your maximum, your willpower and self-discipline cannot push you to move forward. Willpower and self-discipline are fickle and can crumble when you become overwhelmed.

The story of Ned is a great glimpse into what happens when you try to always push yourself to do things that you need to do for success in life. Overcoming the sense of being overwhelmed and overworked is not easy. You have to create an organizational system to make your success consistent even when you're feeling glum and fatigued.

Particularly in business, there will be days when the inertia is too heavy and you don't feel like performing the tasks on your to-do list. There will be tasks that you dread doing and thus can't summon the necessary willpower. And there will even be people who try to block your success, and you may not always have the strength to fight them off.

That is where daily systems come into play.

A system is a set of actions that you consistently perform every day in order to streamline your success and reach your goals. Unlike your self-discipline and willpower, a system organizes you and helps you perform your duties without having to push yourself. Willpower and self-discipline, on the other hand, only offer you strength to force yourself to do things; they do not give you a set way of doing things or a streamlined list of actions to complete.

A system becomes routine so that you do not have to think about what you need to do, but instead you just do it. The key to a system is to work on progress and consistency in your life, as opposed to working on goals. For instance, let's go back to Ned and consider if he had used a time management system to split up tasks and make time for each task. He could have automated things so that he could have gotten all of his tasks done in a timelier manner, with less stress, disorganization, and confusion.

Had Ned implemented a few simple daily systems into his approach to his business, he would have been more successful. Ned relied on his self-discipline too much. He just could not force himself to do so much work on his own. Working at maximum, he burned out and began to fail.

For perspective, a goal is antithetical to a system because goals play a part in systems. Systems are simply ways to make sure you take the actions necessary to reach a goal. They are not limited to one thing at a time, as goals are; instead, they apply to everything you must do in your endeavor. Once you complete one goal, you can move onto the next one easily by simply following your system. Systems will carry you through every single goal you set.

Systems also protect you from failure even if you do not reach a goal. Say your goal for the day is to complete 1000 words of writing for a grant proposal. You use a system to help you get some work done, but you do not reach the 1000-word mark. That is fully acceptable, because you still got some writing done. A system enables you to reach a better place, even if you do not meet your exact goal. From that better place, it is even easier to move forward and accomplish your ultimate goal later on.

Every day is a chance to get closer and closer to your final goal when you have a good system in place.

Ned focused on accomplishing a series of goals each day, such as generating new leads and finishing projects. He did not implement any sort of system that forced him to perform the necessary actions for his goals at a specific time each day. Had he implemented a system and structured his work, he would have been able to tackle his goals in a timely manner instead of working in chaos and exhausting himself. Then his business would have thrived as he earned new clients and pleased old ones simultaneously.

Creating systems begins with having an overall goal in mind. Then you can build the scaffolding that will get you there.

Keep a Scoreboard

The first type of system is to keep a detailed scoreboard for yourself. The heart of this system is that you'll be far more motivated if you feel that you have the possibility to *win* something. You must see some type of gain to fuel interest in the project. Therefore, you want to keep score.

People play at their best when they feel as if they are winning or losing, so be sure to demonstrate how you are progressing and winning. People play differently when they are keeping score. If you're not keeping score, you're just practicing. So start keeping score today to provide automatic motivation for yourself and others. Here are some things you can do to keep a scoreboard.

First, track your progress. Every time you get something done, check it off of your list. Seeing your tasks checked off will give you a sense that you are actually getting something done. A big to-do list on a whiteboard mounted on the wall can help you. This is so motivating because people can visually see they are getting things done, and seeing what they complete makes them realize that the target goal is more and more possible.

Another important element of this system is to celebrate small victories for you and those you are working with whenever you see a victory. The smaller the victory, the better, because it is a chance to motivate yourself and others. This also allows you to have an overall greater number of victories to feel good about and celebrate momentum with. Find every little small victory—be it scoring a new client or finding a way around an obstacle you face. Create friendly competition to boost this concept, even if you have to compete with your own past performance.

Finally, always have an ultimate reward or incentive at the end of the project. When you meet the ultimate goal that you have set, reward yourself. Having some type of reward set up for when you hit your goal can give you something to look forward to, which pushes you forward even when you want to give up. Treat yourself to a spa day when you hit that mark, for example, or treat your team to a night out. This mentality is why bonuses work well to motivate workers in companies.

An example of how to integrate this system into your work life is to create a list of things you wish to accomplish. When you check off an item on the list, have a small celebration, such as a pizza party for the whole team. Be sure to set incentives, such as bonuses or a day trip, at the end. For every sale, you want to mark it and celebrate it. View every day as a chance to rack up more points on your scoreboard.

Time Management

A time management system is essential to success for anyone. Knowing how to divvy up your time and how much time to give to each task will help you complete goals on time. Time management is essential because it really helps you get things done by your deadline, and it provides motivation to follow through on tasks. You can set realistic expectations once you know an approximate time frame for everything you do.

To practice good time management, first set a routine for your work. A routine is a system that enables you to know what to do when. You know you need to start work at nine, for example. Take deadlines and other time commitments into account when setting up your routine. Be sure to set aside time for work, eating, sleep, appointments, and other commitments. In addition, don't neglect yourself or you will hit your maximum and become too stressed to handle work. So be sure to also tend to your health, sleep well, and eat right.

Always assess your time needs on a project. Ask yourself, "How much time will something take?" To get a better idea of your time needs, you can time yourself on certain tasks to get an idea of how long things take you at your normal, comfortable pace. You should never feel hectic or stressed with a good time management system, so be sure to time yourself doing things at a pace that does not stress you out and give yourself some wiggle room for unforeseen issues that may cause you to need more time.

Read over your daily tasks at the start of the day. When you get to work or even when you wake up, look over a planner and see what you have planned for the day. This helps you ensure that you meet goals in a timely manner. Be sure to account time for important appointments, as well as the amount of time you need to do things related to your business, such as answering emails, attending networking events, and having strategy meetings.

Minimize distractions whenever you are working. Focus on one thing at a time. Multitasking and having distractions can drastically cut down on your productivity. Set a specific time to check emails, for example, instead of checking emails throughout the day and letting your inbox distract you from the task at hand. Also have a set time to focus on marketing or on networking.

Lower Your Transaction Costs

Transaction costs is an economic term for the cost you must expend to be in the market.

Whenever you do something, you have some sort of cost associated with it. The cost may be monetary, such as an investment to start a business. Or it may be emotional, such as the apprehension of embarking on a new business opportunity without knowing if you will succeed or fail. Or it could even be physical, demanding your physical prowess and labor. These are simply the costs, or obstacles, you have to overcome to play the game.

Build a system around manipulating these costs to your benefit. Cut out the costs that tax you and make the gains you want convenient and easy.. Make it harder on yourself to do unproductive things, such as procrastinating, by raising the costs that such habits will create for you. Meanwhile, lower the transaction costs on things you want to do more consistently. You want to encourage good habits, such as systematic work and time management, by making them easier for you so that they "cost" less. Meanwhile, flip the tables and make bad habits, like being disorganized, having poor time management, and procrastinating, too expensive to entertain.

For example, by being more organized, you have less stress and spend less time looking for things you need in the office. So that makes it easier to practice this behavior. Find effortless means to organize your office without spending too much money and without taking too much time. Use a simple color coding system for papers and use boxes laying around the house to create paper bins that you label clearly with a Sharpie. This costs almost nothing, yet it saves you so much hassle as you work.

Notice how the behavior of being organized becomes easier with reduced costs and how that good habit makes reaching your goal easier. You just cut down on your costs by reducing the taxation of being disorganized. Plus, you expended almost no money or effort organizing your office.

Make undesired behaviors cost too much. Train yourself to view bad behavior as something that is too expensive to engage in. For example, raise the costs of unproductive behavior by forcing yourself to climb five flights of stairs to smoke or eat chocolate or browse your phone.

Let's look at how to generally manipulate transaction costs. The first part of this is to make good habits cost nothing. The reward must be greater than the cost for a good behavior. This is the only way to motivate yourself to make positive changes. For example, you might make it easier to be organized by spending less money on an organizational system for the office, and you can make it so simple to find things in the office that it reduces stress at work.

Make bad habits cost a lot. You won't want to engage in a bad habit if the costs outweigh the profit. A good example is to reduce unproductivity by making time that you spend not working lose you money.

Consider how Ned could have reduced his transaction costs. The amount of work he put into his business became too much for him to handle alone and he quickly hit his maximum, where he could not function anymore. By making work easier and being disorganized harder, he could have made his life and work much more efficient. He should have made his bad habits (working 12-hour days) too expensive for him to afford and his good habits (organization) practically effortless.

Gather All Information First

This system is about gathering everything you require for a project before you even start the project. Find the information that is critical to the project and try to complete your research phase all in one go. This system saves you the time of trying to gather resources while you are immersed in your project. You can focus on the project rather than on gathering resources and information. This removes the hurdles that halt momentum.

You can use momentum to roll forward, making the project easier to perform as you are in the middle of it. Having to stop your work to find out information or find a supply can kill momentum. Momentum is when you work without stopping, letting each completed goal build on top of each other to make the next goal easier to complete.

For example, before a big work project, you may need a team of people with certain skills or a single partner. You may need some basic supplies or a specific software. Even consider the office supplies you will need, such as pens and paper, and have them at hand. Gather all of the resources you need and have them ready before you even commence working. Also, list all of the information you will need before working, such as contact information for other workers and the deadline, so that you do not have to search for this information while you are busy. Think of it like carrying all the groceries out of your car in one trip.

In Kerry Patterson's book *Crucial Conversations,* he suggests some of the information you must gather or assess before you embark on any project.

Assign responsibility. Ask "Who is responsible for what?" Assign a name to each task that must be completed. This is essential for creating clarity. You want to have a leader, a person in charge of budgeting, a person in charge of marketing, a person in charge of human resources, and so on. For every aspect of your project, find someone who can handle it. If you are handling everything by yourself because you are working solo, then delegate responsibility to yourself by splitting your tasks into different roles and then performing each of those roles separately at different times to ensure you complete them.

Specify your desired outcome and expectations. Be very specific about what you want to accomplish and what you expect to do. Having a target outcome can guide you in success by making it clear to you what tasks you have to complete and how you need to work. Specify how much work you want to get done, how many units you want to sell, how much money you want to make, and when you want to meet your goals by. Go ahead and set clear goals that are both reachable and inspiring. For example, you may want to look at previous sales and say, "Okay, we sold 1000 units last month. Let's hit 1200 this month!"

Determine the deadline. You probably have a deadline set by your boss or client. If you don't, set one yourself. Nothing will motivate you like a specific date when you must have a project completed by. Deadlines can give you a clear guideline for how to structure your time and when to meet milestones. Make sure to set a realistic deadline—do not promise someone the moon and then not be able to deliver. You want to set a deadline that gives you plenty of room to complete something by, taking into account potential setbacks and challenges that cost you time.

Have a follow-up plan. You don't want to think of your current goal as the finish line because life goes on after you reach the goal.

What happens after the project? What do you do next? Have a plan for the steps to take once you complete a project and what goals to move on to. This can motivate you as you have more things to look forward to.

Also consider following.

Gather physical resources. You will need different things to get something done—money, people, software, office supplies, materials. Find out what you need and obtain all of it.

Identify obstacles. Knowing the obstacles beforehand can help you determine how to mitigate them. People will have a ton of enthusiasm when they brainstorm ideas; they see only sunshine and are eager to press on. When unexpected obstacles arise, however, their enthusiasm runs out and inertia sets in. If everyone involved knows what to expect and thinks of these obstacles as hurdles to overcome as a team, then morale will not be so heavily impacted. If you see no obstacles in your path, you need to brainstorm more to account for potential pitfalls.

Back to our example of poor Ned. Imagine how much easier things would have been for him if he had organized his resources and gathered information first. First, he should have organized his office, putting notes where it would be easy to find them when he needed them. Next, he should have found the software programs that would have let him automate emails, newsletters, quotes, and invoices, which would have lessened the workload he carried by himself. Finally, he should have anticipated the volume of work coming in so that he could have managed his time better and handled his workload more efficiently. He should have set deadlines and made sure to meet them. He could have considered hiring someone else to take on some of his responsibility had he estimated how much work he was going to gain.

On top of that, he should have identified challenges and prepared for them, such as having too great of a workload. Then he could have mitigated these challenges with a bit of forethought. Gathering all of these resources beforehand could have saved Ned so much work after he launched his business.

Daily systems streamline work and cut down on the amount of willpower you require to plug on in life. They make actions systematic and therefore they encourage progress. You can avoid failure in your life by using systems to implement efficiency and forward progress. Don't be a Ned. Use daily systems to propel yourself into success.

Takeaways:

- Systems are sets of daily behaviors. It doesn't have to be more complex than that. Systems stand in stark contrast to goals because goals are one-off accomplishments, while systems emphasize consistency and long-term success.
- Keep a scoreboard for everything large and trivial. This keeps you motivated and striving toward growth and progress.

- Manage your time better by understanding how long things will take in reality and accounting for your own quirks and inefficiencies.
- Lower your transaction costs by making undesirable behaviors inconvenient and unwieldy while making desirable behaviors convenient and easy.
- Gather all of the information and materials you need all at once and before you get started. This allows you to work interruption-free and gather momentum.

Summary Guide

Chapter 1. Stop Thinking, Just Execute

- The art of following through is something that allows you to create the life that you actually want instead of settling for the life you currently have.
- It can be said to be composed of four parts: focus, self-discipline, action, and persistence—all equally important.
- However, it's not just as easy as knowing you have to do it and thus doing it. There are powerful reasons we don't finish what we start and follow through very often. These reasons can generally be split into two camps: inhibiting tactics and psychological roadblocks.
- Inhibiting tactics are the ways we plan against ourselves without even realizing it. They include (1) setting bad goals, (2) procrastination, (3) indulging in temptations and distractions, and (4) poor time management.

- Psychological roadblocks are the ways we don't follow through because we are unconsciously protecting ourselves. These include (1) laziness and lack of discipline, (2) fear of judgment, rejection, and failure, (3) perfectionism out of insecurity, and (4) lack of self-awareness.

Chapter 2: Staying Hungry

- How do we stay hungry and motivated? By delving deep and really asking what internal and external motivators you have at your disposal—a task that is rarely performed.
- External motivators are when we leverage other people, places, and things to push us into action. For the most part, these are when we want to avoid negative consequences involving other people, places, and things. These methods include accountability partners and groups, putting money down upfront, and self-bribery.
- Internal motivators are when we look at how we stand to benefit and improve

our lives. These are universal needs, drives, and desires that are easy to lose track of. The easy way to find these is to answer a set of questions that directly asks things such as *how am I going to benefit from this* and *how does my life stand to improve from this*? It's only through answering these questions that you realize what you are neglecting.

- Anything we want to accomplish has an associated opportunity cost. We must sacrifice, even if we are sacrificing our ability to lie on the couch and watch television. We can deal with this mental obstacle by playing with the cost-benefit ratio so the cost is minimized or the benefit is maximized.
- Motivation has been shown to work best when we are reminded of it—otherwise, out of sight, out of mind. Thus, you should have cues you're your motivations all around you—but make sure to keep them distinct and memorable, use all five senses (even taste), and make sure to change and switch them periodically to avoid

growing used to them and forgetting them.

Chapter 3: Create a Manifesto

- A manifesto is nothing more than a set of rules to follow every day. We might hate rules, but rules take the guesswork out of our days and give us guidelines to follow. They make matters black and white, which is helpful to following through because there is simply no other choice.
- Rule 1: Are you acting out of laziness? If so, is this a characterization you want about yourself?
- Rule 2: Three major tasks a day, maximum. Differentiate between important tasks, urgent tasks, and simple wasted motion.
- Rule 3: Create daily limitations and requirements for yourself. These keep you within the bounds of what you know you need to do. These are also the building blocks of good habits.
- Rule 4: Sometimes we lose sight of what we want to accomplish. Thus, reaffirm

your intentions by stating "I want," "I will," and "I won't" statements.

- Rule 5: Try to look into the future, 10 minutes, hours, and days at a time. Do you like what you see when you consider not following through? Is it worth the benefit to the current self at the expense of the future self? Probably not.
- Rule 6: It's just 10 minutes, right? So if you want to quit, it's just 10 minutes. And if you need to wait, it's just 10 minutes.

Chapter 4: Follow-Through Mindsets

- Following through is 100% mental, which means it's probably a good idea to talk about the mindsets you attempt to embody.
- Mindset 1: It's all worthwhile. If you feel that your hard work will get you somewhere, you belong and are as good as anyone else, and you feel impact toward your overall goals, execution is easier to stick with.
- Mindset 2: Become comfortable with discomfort. Everything you want to do

will have elements of discomfort, unless you just want to watch television all day by yourself. Thus, becoming used to this feeling allows you to tackle what you want without fear.

- Mindset 3: Without following through, there is no learning. Only when you finish something can you evaluate yourself and correct your errors. Embody an information-gathering mindset.

- Mindset 4: The detrimental power of stress and anxiety can't be overstated. Even being in a poor mood is dangerous to your productivity and follow-through. Be aware and take proactive measures to modulate your stress levels.

Chapter 5: The Science of Smashing Procrastination

- Tackling procrastination is similar to pushing Sisyphus's stone. You can beat it back for a bit, but it's so natural that you will never be fully rid of it. The problem is typified by time inconsistency, where we comprise two selves that don't have overlapping desires—one wants gratification in the future and the other wants it right now.

- Temptation bundling is an effective method to battle procrastination. It consists of combining your unpleasurable tasks with something pleasurable. This mainly works because you are battling time inconsistency and giving both selves what they want simultaneously.

- Start easy and small. Procrastination thrives off inertia. Therefore, you need to make the path to motion and action as easy as possible. Then eventually you can gain momentum—the opposite of inertia.

- Sometimes beating procrastination just requires a kick in the pants. Fear and productive paranoia can do that to you— if you are so fearful of the negative repercussions you will face, then you will certainly be spurred into action. But this is not a method to use very frequently.

Chapter 6. No Distraction Zone

- Minimize your distractions in your environment. It turns out that out of sight is out of mind with distractions, so don't keep anything stimulating near your workstation otherwise your willpower will slowly deplete itself.
- Create default actions wherever possible. This is where the easiest and lowest resistance past for you is the path you want the most. This is also done through curating and designing your environment for productivity.
- Singletasking is an important concept because it definitively proves the flaws of multitasking. When you switch from task to task, you create attention residue. This means it takes a while for you to adjust to each new task, even if you were already familiar with it. You can eliminate this by singletasking, and also by batching, which is when you do all similar types of tasks together to capitalize on your mental efficiency.
- A don't-do list can be just as powerful as a to-do list because we are rarely told what to ignore. As a result, these distractions or sneaky time-suckers can

invade our space without us even knowing we are being duped. Include tasks you can't move forward on, make progress on, or help.

- The 40–70 rule is when you beat inaction through the amount of information you seek. If you have less than 40%, don't act. But if you have 70%, you must act. You'll never have 100%, and chances are, 70% is more than sufficient—the rest you learn along the way, anyway.

- Finally, you might want to do nothing from time to time. This is rest and relaxation—but you should think of it as mental recovery. What does an athlete do between races or matches? You got it—they recover so they are primed to work again when necessary.

Chapter 7: Deadly Pitfalls

- Pitfalls to following through and finishing what you start? Too many to name. But a select few in this chapter are stronger and more dangerous than most.

- False hope syndrome is when you expect that you will be able to change or improve to an unrealistic degree. When you inevitably fail to meet this mark, there is a very real backlash that results in you being even less motivated and disciplined than before you started. To beat this, set proper expectations based on your history and understand the difference between goals and expectations.

- Overthinking is sneaky because it feels like action and it even feels productive. But it's not. Overthinking is when you fixate and can't seem to take the first step toward action. Zero in on the details that matter, deliberately ignore everything else, and you'll feel much more clarity.

- Worrying is when you fixate on something and inevitably start drawing out the negative scenarios and pitfalls. However, worrying is also when you fixate on things you can't control while ignoring what you can control—the present. The solution is to focus on what you can do right now and only right now.

- Do you know yourself? Well, what about in terms of productivity and how you work and produce the best? You can consider time of day, environment, setting, and so on. But you should consider that knowing yourself is also the ability to look at yourself and understand why you may have failed or come up short. It is the ability to self-diagnose and be self-aware.

Chapter 8. Daily Systems for Success

- Systems are sets of daily behaviors. It doesn't have to be more complex than that. Systems stand in stark contrast to goals because goals are one-off accomplishments, while systems emphasize consistency and long-term success.
- Keep a scoreboard for everything large and trivial. This keeps you motivated and striving toward growth and progress.
- Manage your time better by understanding how long things will take

in reality and accounting for your own quirks and inefficiencies.

- Lower your transaction costs by making undesirable behaviors inconvenient and unwieldy while making desirable behaviors convenient and easy.

- Gather all of the information and materials you need all at once and before you get started. This allows you to work interruption-free and gather moment.